Two Ways To An End

Larry Babka

New Genesis Publishing, LLC
Scottsdale, Arizona

Two Ways To An End

Copyright 2009 by Larry Babka
All rights reserved

ISBN 978-0-615-32878-2
This book or parts thereof may not be reproduced in any form, stored electronically, or transmitted in any form by any means without the written permission of the publisher, except as provided by the United States of America copyright law.

Published by: New Genesis Publishing, LLC
Scottsdale, AZ 85254
Phone 602-595-2285
Email: info@twowaystoanend.com

Published in association with and distributed by;
InterMedia Publishing Group
www.intermediapub.com
623-337-8710

Editing by Glori Nuessle, Doug Milligan, Doug Coke, and other friends and family members
Cover design and page layout by Kimberly Sarmento
Cover illustration by Matthew Attard

Scriptures taken from the *Holy Bible*, New International Version
Copyright 1985 by The Zondervan Corporation
Copyright by International Bible Society

Printed in the United States of America

www.twowaystoanend.com

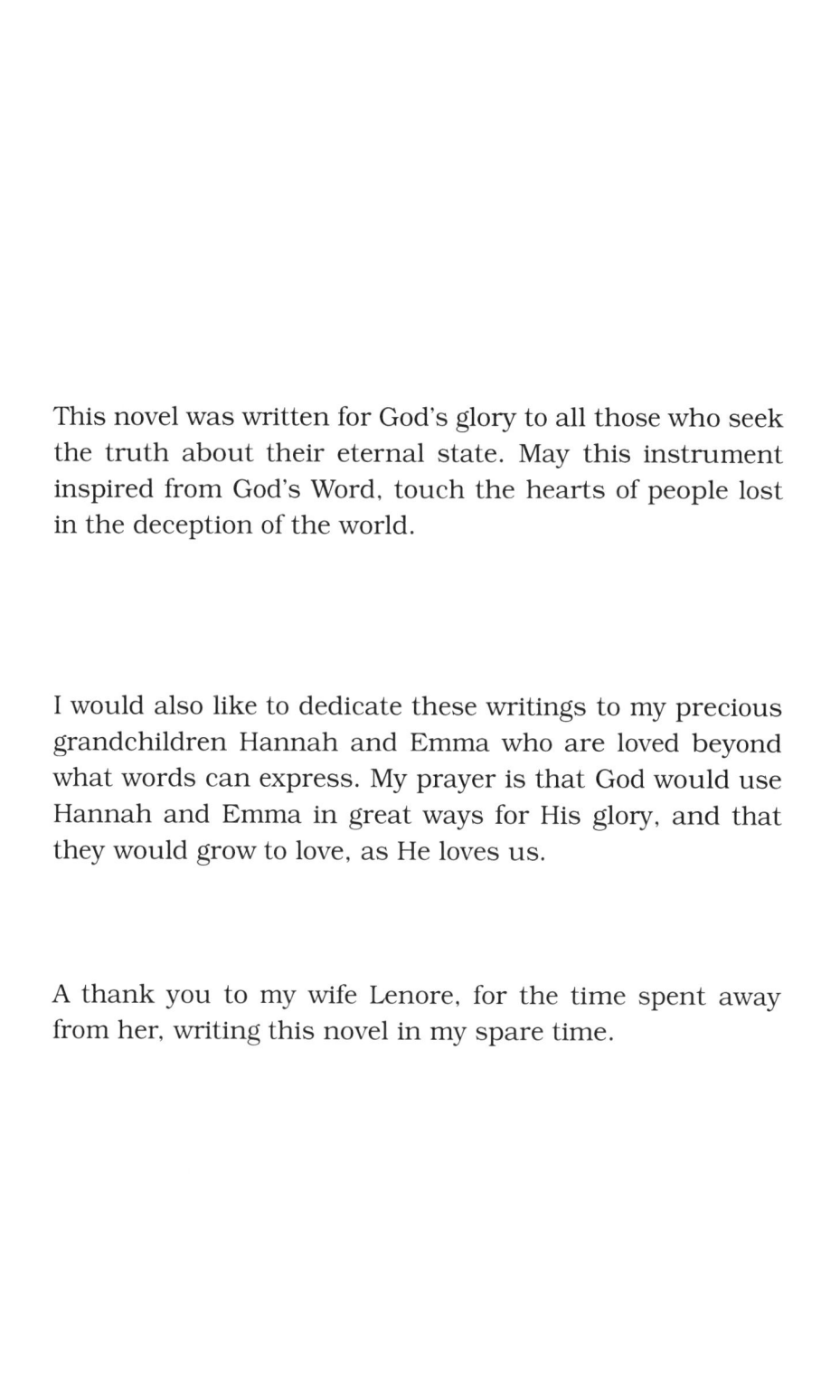

This novel was written for God's glory to all those who seek the truth about their eternal state. May this instrument inspired from God's Word, touch the hearts of people lost in the deception of the world.

I would also like to dedicate these writings to my precious grandchildren Hannah and Emma who are loved beyond what words can express. My prayer is that God would use Hannah and Emma in great ways for His glory, and that they would grow to love, as He loves us.

A thank you to my wife Lenore, for the time spent away from her, writing this novel in my spare time.

CONTENTS

    Preface 9
1. In The Beginning 13
2. The Discovery 25
3. The Diagnosis 34
4. Relationships 43
5. Passing 53
6. Heavens Gate 61
7. The Throne Of God 73
8. Call to Art 81
9. Pulling The Plug 89
10. Rob's Memorial Service 103
11. Banquet 111
12. Mansion 118
13. Hell 125
14. Why 133
15. Angels and Demons 139
16. The Trinity 146
17. Creation 155
18. Universe 164
19. The Rapture 174
20. Time With Mom 182
21. Every Knee Will Bow 189
22. Time With Dad 194
23. New Earth 207
24. Art's Memorial Service 216
25. The Letter 224
26. Ending Well 243
27. Looking Back 247
    Epilogue 250

PREFACE

Almost everyone has some curiosity about the existence of life after death. Our interest over these mysteries, and their ultimate understanding, is written in every human's heart by God Himself.

If you've picked up this book, chances are you have wrestled with and wondered about what happens when you die physically. It is also possible that you've heard about the book from someone who cares about your eternal destiny. Regardless of how or why you are reading this book, I am confident that you will find revelation and security in understanding God's plan for you here on earth, and then, in the eternal life that is to come.

This is a story about two brothers, whom God loved equally, and unconditionally. These two lives were lived in very different ways. They reflect the reality of the consequences of a life on the right path as contrasted with one on the wrong path. Their choices made before their death in this present world determined their destination in the world to come. These two outcomes sum up the eventual eternal outcome of every living soul, past, present, and future. This story reflects the path that leads to fulfillment and purpose, as opposed to one lived selfishly. It is my prayer that the lessons learned through these lives will impact the reader in a significant way.

My name is Reveal, an angel of God, and I have been privileged to witness the events written in this book. It has been my assignment from God to watch over Rob, the main character in this story. As a messenger and guardian, I have been by his side as God directed me during his entire life on earth, and now in Heaven. It has only been a few months since Rob passed from his physical life on earth into his spiritual state, which is eternal.

Rob's story will capture your imagination and expand your understanding of God. The examination of Rob's story will inspire the reader to think and reflect on the destiny that awaits all humanity. It is Rob's prayer that your view of the realm that is to come will impact you in a special way. As a messenger of God himself, I can testify that everything expressed here will bring you closer to God and to an understanding of the afterlife we will all experience.

The writer of this book was given divine revelation through my witness, and the Spirit that lives within him, in recording these events. These words were placed in the heart and mind of this writer for reflection and contemplation.

Rob, the main character in this story, asked that these events be recorded, telling the story of his life. He has sent me to convey his message as an encouragement, and a warning, from an eternal perspective.

I have seen Rob's life unfold before me as God directed my assignment. As his guardian, Rob was protected from the warfare that occurred in another dimension against the forces of darkness. I've watched over him from the beginning, and have grown to love him as God loves him. His story although unique, has common threads that are woven in everyone's life.

Because he was chosen by God to share his story, I was

given authority to reveal these events for God's greater purposes. It has been my joy to be used by God for this unique work. Rob's life on earth was special, and I was privileged to be a part of it.

Some of the events during Rob's life would have destroyed and/or injured him, if God hadn't altered his circumstances and protected him. His well being was entrusted to me by God, and I protected him without altering his free will in choosing his path. I appeared to Rob on several occasions without his knowledge, manifested in the form of a man to convey or reveal a truth that would be vital or beneficial to his path. God granted me special abilities for His specific purposes as Rob's life played out.

The basis for this book revolves around a letter written to Rob's brother, Art. His letter conveys the heart of God as he articulates his love for him and the foundations for his eternal destiny. Rob is hopeful that all humankind would read his letter, and be changed by it. Rob also wants you to know, although he wrote the letter to his brother, God has told him that his letter is for all humanity and expresses His heart for everyone.

Understanding your eternal state is a difficult undertaking. Let me explain a good allegory about humankind's inability to understand these places unseen by the physical world. The human race on earth is much like a society who, if you can imagine, are all born blind. None in the society have ever had sight. Then one day, someone from another world appears who can see.

No matter how much the man who is able to see tries to describe what he sees, the people without sight are unable to perceive those descriptions. Humanity is much like that society; they are unable to understand something outside their limited world. There is a place that is more wonderful than you are able to comprehend, and another place, much worse than anyone could imagine.

The choices that exist in accepting truth over deception are real. This book presents truth and testimony so that no man would perish. For those who scoff at an afterlife, please investigate for yourself the realities that lie before you. Eventually, every person will die a physical death. Everyone understands that reality. It is one's view of eternity that determines a person's eternal destiny.

Please consider carefully as you read these pages the reality of God's existence. He has supreme authority in all things. Consider the joy that can be found in a right relationship with Him. Rob's desire is that his recorded experiences will be received by the reader as it was intended, in love.

May you be blessed and changed by the grace and love of an awesome God. To God who created everything and everyone in the universe, may He be glorified in this work.

In the Beginning

As Rob sat looking at a photo of the family six months earlier over Christmas, he couldn't help but think about how blessed he was to have spent the past six months preparing them for his departure. He knew that his weakening condition would soon end his life and leave them only with their memories of him. Rob knew that his family would miss him, but they were prepared for his departure and would have their memories of him for comfort. He was now ready to pass from this life to another, where he would live eternally. His thoughts about heaven seemed to consume him, as he drifted in and out of sleep.

Rob's wife Kate was prepared for Rob's passing and just wanted Rob to go comfortably. Rob had everything prepared, and Kate knew that she would someday join him in heaven. Rob made the transition with the family as joyful as possible, under the circumstances. Kate knew that the sooner Rob passed, the less suffering he would endure.

When Kate came in and saw Rob staring at the Christmas photos, she asked if he remembered how excited he was when the kids opened their presents. Rob was dozing in and out of sleep, but he was remembering all the festivities and events that lead him to this point. Rob tried his best to remember all that had happened. Then he fell into a light sleep, as he remembered that wonderful time with his family.

Six months earlier.

The sights and smell of the Christmas season were at their peak as Rob set out for the mall for his annual gift hunt. It was a typical crisp winter morning in the Chicago suburb of Wheaton, Illinois. A few wispy snowflakes cascaded down enhancing the seasonal ambiance. As Rob got out of his Suburban, he felt invigorated and joyful. This year Christmas Eve fell on a Friday, and the stores were jammed with last minute shoppers. Rob loved the crowds and the excitement in the air.

Rob's annual shopping excursion on Christmas Eve had become a tradition, as he bought gifts for his family and friends. He loved finding crazy things that would surprise those he loved. The stores were bustling with frantic shoppers who were desperate to finish. Rob savored the looking and made it an adventure as he scoured the stores for each perfect gift.

Rob always shopped on Christmas Eve to take advantage of last minute sales and promotions. As usual, his spirits were high. He diligently hunted for that special gift for each person. Rob found a soft plush cover-up for his wife, Kate. She always seemed to be cold, so as Rob felt the velvety surface, he knew Kate would use it often. As he ran his hands across the luxurious surface, he could see her snuggling up in the soft folds of the blanket in their family room.

Rob's daughter loved cooking, and Rob knew she was saving for an automated bread maker. Rob did extensive research to determine the best manufacturer and model. He was surprised by the variety and choices and settled on one that had all the automated features that would cut down on the time needed to prepare and bake the fresh bread. With the busy activities of the two kids, Rob knew having the enhanced features would help with her busy schedule.

The highlight of his shopping was finding the perfect gift for Jen, his 10 year old granddaughter, and David his 8 year old grandson. Each year, he made sure that his gift would be one that they could enjoy together. Rob's love of winter activities generally lead him to items that enhanced their winter fun together.

Rob knew that their tattered ice skates were getting too tight for them to continue to wear. They were growing quickly and every other year, they seemed to grow out of them. His friend, Aaron owned the local sporting goods store and always gave him a good deal on the ice skates. He knew his gift would be predictable, because he always gave them new skates for Christmas. The kids seemed to love it because it was so much fun skating with Papa. That's what they liked calling him.

When he walked through the doors, he noticed a beautiful toboggan on display in the center of the store. The wood was shiny and rich with color. The length was six feet, perfect for three or four depending on the rider's size. As he lifted the end and ran his hands over the smooth basswood, thoughts of his fifty year old toboggan made him realize how tattered and beaten up it had gotten. The basswood bottom was so smooth, and there was a padded interior to cushion the shock which was perfect for an old guy like himself. Rob could visualize himself and the kids flying down the Forest Preserve hill screaming at the higher speed the new toboggan would bring.

His impulse to buy the toboggan got the best of him, and the next thing he knew he was at the checkout with a boxed toboggan that a clerk brought from the back of the store. Rob began to feel guilty because deep down, he knew the gift was more for him than it was for his grandchildren. The cost was much higher than he was expecting to spend, and he figured the skates could wait till the next year; he ignored his selfishness and checked out. On the way home, Rob's guilt kept increasing until he finally gave in, and turned around to buy the ice skates for each of them, as he originally set out to do. After purchasing the ice skates, Rob was so excited that he set out to return home.

Rob completely forgot about the other gifts he intended to buy from the mall down the street. When he pulled into the driveway, Kate was there as he unloaded the large unmarked box from the back of the Suburban.

"What's that?" Kate asked.

"Nothing," he replied as he tried to hide the box quickly in the garage.

Rob would never let anyone see his gifts before they were given out on Christmas Day, and Rob was not expecting Kate to be home until later.

The large box really aroused her curiosity, as she pressed him to tell her what it contained. Rob knew that Kate couldn't keep a secret and now that she saw the large box, she would be calling their daughter Laura to see if she had any clues about what was in the large box. After several tries to extract information about the box from Rob, Kate went in the house to call Laura. She was also clueless and couldn't imagine what would be in such a large box. They continued to guess what it was for several minutes before finally giving up.

Rob was busy wrapping the toboggan in the garage. He

kept plenty of rolls of Christmas paper insuring that no present would be seen before the big day. Each year, he would buy his supplies just after Christmas when wrapping paper was discounted drastically. The garage was locked up, and he always proclaimed the space "off limits" to the family until after Christmas.

Rob locked the door to the unattached garage as he wrapped the large box before Kate noticed the small manufacturer's name and model number stenciled on the side. The rolls of paper would not cover any one panel, so the box was a checkerboard of various papers that looked odd but festive. Rob also wrapped the skates and Kate's beautiful blanket before leaving the garage to let Kate know he needed to run a few errands.

Rob remembered that he hadn't finished shopping. He pulled out his list and saw that several people were missed. He went into the house and told Kate that he had missed a few gifts because he couldn't drive around with the large box in the back of the Suburban. He asked if it would be okay to finish up and meet her later. Kate was surprised that Rob had come home so early in the first place because, each year, he generally shopped until late in the afternoon or early evening. She knew how Rob would never relax until all his little gifts were bought and wrapped. She told Rob to go ahead as she was going to her daughter Laura's house to help bake some cookies.

Kate figured that she might as well make herself productive while Rob focused on finishing his shopping and gift wrapping for the season. She knew Laura would have her hands full with the kid's activities and could use her help. Rob would probably be back around 7:00, and she would plan to be home when he returned. Rob had most of his gifts selected ahead of time, as he spent weeks searching the internet for the best deals. His list was long and detailed, and every gift was special. As evening came, Rob knew that he was running out of time; he finished up so he could wrap the gifts before Kate came home.

Rob played Christmas music in the garage as he finished wrapping and labeling his gifts. He couldn't wait until the kids opened the large box with the toboggan. He knew that they loved to go tobogganing almost as much as he did each year. As he was ready to exit the garage, he noticed his old tattered toboggan hanging on the side wall. As he looked at it with a sense of loss, he realized that over the years, most of the varnish had worn off and there were fractures in many of the planks. Memories of him and his brother receiving the toboggan as a child filled his heart. The toboggan had looked much like the new one he had just purchased. He remembered the excitement as he and his brother unwrapped it one Christmas morning.

Thoughts of him and his brother and then the times with his family raced through his head. He reminisced about his daughter growing up made him realize how special she was to him. She loved the winter activities almost as much as he did, and would often go with he and the grandkids. Now the grandchildren seemed to have that same special passion for tobogganing. As winter approached, it was the topic of most conversations.

This year's winter had been very strange, because each time it snowed; the snow would turn into a misty rain leaving a crust on the accumulated surface. But now, the weather forecast called for snow on Christmas and continuing the entire next week as a large front moved in. Rob was so excited when he heard the forecast; his exuberance was second only to the joy he would feel on Christmas day when the family would gather for fellowship and gift giving.

Even as a young child, Rob loved giving gifts more than receiving them. Sometimes he would save all year long to just buy the perfect gift for someone he had in his heart. One year he gave his brother Art an electric guitar, that Art secretly wanted. Rob worked a paper route all year to buy it. The look on his brother's face was all the reward Rob needed when his brother opened the box with the guitar. Rob loved his brother, and he was the center of Rob's life growing up. They did everything together.

As Rob grew older, his mom would say; "Rob will never grow up completely, because he longs for the days of adventure that he once had with his brother."

Often times, Rob would sit looking out into space as his mind relived the grand days of excitement and fun with his brother. Kate would sometimes find him sitting silently as he thought about how much he missed him.

It was over twenty years since Art moved to New York. As the years passed, the relationship seemed to fade away. Rob wondered if Art ever thought about him and their childhood days. He knew that even though they were apart, the memories were there for them to remember. No one could take the rich thoughts that filled Rob's mind away. The memories were bittersweet, knowing that they shared so much together when they were young. But the cares of the world, and the lures of life, kept them separated and distant.

It was nearly 7:00 when Kate finally came home to find Rob silently sitting in his easy chair staring into space. Rob didn't hear her come in and as she saw him there, she knew he was thinking about his brother. She could always tell when Rob would tear up as he reminisced about days gone by.

Kate came, leaned over and kissed him on his cheek. Rob was surprised by the warm soft touch, but it was just what he needed at that moment.

Kate gently knelt down and softly asked, "Are you thinking about Art?"

Rob nodded and said, "I wish he were here with us for

Christmas. I miss him Kate."

"Rob, let's call him tomorrow before the family gathers to wish him a merry Christmas," Kate replied.

"Thanks Kate, but we both know he won't pick up; he never does."

Kate had stopped at Blockbusters, to rent a movie to watch, as they always did each year on Christmas Eve. They would alternate picking the movie, and this year, it was Kate's turn. The movie had to be one that revolved around Christmas. Kate picked, "It's A Wonderful Life". Last year, Rob picked "Miracle on 34th Street" for the third time. As the years went by, most of the movies were repeaters and they had already been seen at least once, but they never grew tired of watching a great classic movie that was inspiring. As Kate prepared some popcorn, Rob built a fire to set the mood for the movie. Their cozy "Rec. Room" enhanced the experience as they snuggled up on the sofa.

As the movie ended, they were both wiping their eyes. Rob looked at Kate and asked if she thought their lives really had an impact on others. Kate smiled and pulled him in closer for a hug. "Rob, I think much more than we will ever know. If I didn't have you as my husband, life wouldn't be the same. Your love for people inspires us all."

Rob then looked at Kate and said, "Sometimes it's hard to see if what you do makes any difference, but when I look at you, it makes me realize that it's the little things that I've seen you do. For instance, tonight when you came in and saw that I needed a loving touch, that's what makes such a difference to me."

Rob continued to look at her and said, "I am so happy that we found one another and that through all our hard times and the times that seemed hopeless, we stuck with it, and committed to one another. Thank you for staying with me even when I didn't deserve your love."

"No Rob," Kate replied, "thank you for being the best you could as a husband and a father and more than that, thank you for loving God and His Word. Your devotion and example has been a model for us all."

That night as they retired to their bedroom, they both were thinking and talking about the closeness of their family and how they loved the kids. As they cuddled together and fell into a deep sleep, sweet dreams entered their minds, and they felt content and at peace. Rob had dreams of the new toboggan, as it raced down the Forest Preserve hill with the grandkids as they were laughing and screaming with delight from the thrill.

The next morning, Rob woke up as usual before the sun was up.

Kate saw him stirring and pulled him in for a hug. "Can't you sleep in for a change?" she asked.

Rob tried to lay there for a few minutes, but finally gave in to the draw of a new day. He slipped out of bed and into the kitchen. The smell of freshly brewed coffee filled the kitchen as he let their dog Ginger out into the back yard.

Rob then settled in to his morning study time, as he read the Bible and prayed for his family and friends. Rob made this time each day special, and as the years passed, he grew closer and closer to God. His time alone with God ignited each day in a special way and made him content.

After an hour, Rob started the shower and brushed his teeth as the water warmed. As Rob lifted his arm to shave in the shower, a pain shot up his arm. The daily pain medication to control his arthritis would take over in an hour as the effects set in. Rob figured it was his usual battle with the debilitating disease that began to surface five years earlier. As the years went by, the pain steadily increased and his joints swelled and stiffened.

Rob felt very sore as he got dressed after the hot shower.

The pain in his arm still throbbed each time he lifted it. Rob had a hard time focusing on the impending joy that the day would bring him, as it had each year when the family arrived. The morning seemed to be flying by, and Rob needed to get all the gifts from the garage into the house.

As he put on his coat and stepped out into the cold crisp air, an invigorating feeling came over him, making the pain disappear. There was a very light snow falling that made Rob smile in anticipation of the fun coming on the great hill a few miles away. As he entered the garage, he thought, "How will I get the toboggan in the house?" He remembered that he bought a new dolly recently that had a platform perfect for transporting awkward items on it.

The pain really grabbed him as he tried to pick up the large package and put it on the dolly. As he wiggled it on the platform, the paper tore leaving the stenciled manufacturer of the toboggan visible. Rob decided to add another patch of paper with a dense pattern so it would be impossible to read the box. Rob knew that they would all be speculating about the contents of the box. It would ruin his fun if they were to discover what was in the box. Allowing them to try and guess what it was, always intensified the drama. Each year, Rob would make the guessing part of the fun before the gifts were opened. He would often put small items in large packages and disguise the packaging to fool them.

He finally maneuvered it into the house; it was all he could do to slide the large box across the floor in front of the large Christmas tree. The smell of pine from the fresh tree that he cut down the weekend before Christmas made the room smell fresh and appealing. The eclectic array of beautiful ornaments that he and Kate collected over the years and the multi-colored lights, made the warmth of the room cozy and inviting.

Rob knew that if Kate found out about the pain, she

would insist on him seeing a doctor right away. Rob hated going to the doctor and avoided visits at all cost. He knew that it was almost a year since his last visit, and it was inevitable that he would need to make an appointment to renew his prescription medications. But the longer he could put it off, the better it was as far as he was concerned.

Kate woke up about an hour later and cooked bacon and omelets. The smell of bacon filled the house making Rob's stomach growl. Rob wasn't very helpful in the kitchen, and Kate would often chase him out when he tried to help because he always made a big mess in the process. She would often accuse him of making the mess so he wouldn't be asked to help. Rob never denied the plot, and they just left it at that.

After breakfast Rob and Kate headed off to church as they did each year on Christmas Day. Rob loved the annual Christmas service, because it was presented in a more traditional tone than the normal contemporary services. It brought back memories of his childhood when his parents would take them to the small Protestant Church on Christmas Eve. The feeling of the season always made him feel warm and loved.

On the way to church, Kate kept trying to guess what was inside the large box. She never came close to guessing the content and it tickled Rob every time she guessed. The banter went on all the way to the church and left Kate frustrated, because she could never guess any of Rob's gifts. The ride was short and as they entered the church, all their friends greeted them and wished them a merry Christmas. They made it into the worship center and found their seats in the area they preferred before the crowd came.

Rob's kids were always late and as usual, came rushing in as the music was playing. Kate always saved them seats next to them. The service was beautiful and blessed the start of their special day.

The pain in Rob's arm had been reduced from the prescription pain medicine, and he momentarily forgot about it. As Rob and the family spent some time in fellowship after the service, the pain began to return. He wondered if he should have Kate look at his arm, he knew she would make more out of it than he was willing to hear. Her nursing experience, combined with her ongoing concern about Rob's arthritis made Rob feel like he had a terminal illness. So, he decided to wait and see if it would go away on its own.

Rob was quiet on the way back to the house, and Kate sensed something was up.

"Why so quiet?" she asked.

"Just thinking about the family and how we're getting older. I just don't seem to have the energy I used to have especially on Christmas," Rob replied.

Kate smiled and said, "Can't act like a little boy anymore?" "I guess you could say that," he replied.

Kate slid over and kissed him on the cheek as she whispered "you still look like the boy I first married, and regardless of how old you get, I'll always see you that way."

The Discovery

Rob made it home a few minutes before the kids, coming directly from church. Rob's daughter Laura gathered the grandkids out of Sunday school and after a few brief conversations with their friends, left church for Rob's house. They were all excited about spending the day together.

The grandkids came running in when they saw Rob sitting in his easy chair. Rob was trying to act like there wasn't anything wrong. The kids loved hugging him, and they rushed to sit on his lap. The pain from under his upper arm was still intense. Rob knew severe pain was common as a result of his arthritic condition. He figured it would pass soon. It was all he could do to let them cuddle and embrace him momentarily.

Then Kate's mom, Claire, and Rob's Uncle Jim came. They brought along with them their nephews and nieces. Rob loved having what remained of their small family over for the holidays. Rob wished his parents were there to see the grandkids. He really loved having them over for the holidays. Their deaths five years earlier left a void in Rob's life that seemed to escalate over the holidays. It was amazing, how quickly after his dad died, that his mom joined him. It was as if they couldn't be separated from one another.

As he thought about them not being there to enjoy Christmas with them, he realized how much he missed them. Knowing that they were both with the Lord in heaven, his sadness was replaced with happiness. Thinking that they were there together, and that it was a far better place than this, gave Rob comfort. He wondered if they could see the family from heaven celebrating there together.

Rob's Uncle Charlie was struggling with a heart condition similar to his dad's before he died, and it was all he could do to walk from the car to the sofa where he planted himself. He would sit and reminisce about the years of fun with his wife. His wife died ten years earlier, and Rob made sure that he and his children spent the holidays together.

Charlie's son Jim was there with his three kids. Rob felt bad for him, because his wife suddenly decided that raising kids wasn't for her, and abandoned them. Rob helped him through the tough times, and Jim eventually accepted the trial as he leaned on the Lord for comfort.

Rob knew that Jim's strong relationship with God would sustain him through the trial. If it were not for that, he might have not made it through the hardship. The hardest part of it was that he loved his wife so deeply and adored her. Fortunately, he recently met and started dating a sweet girl from the singles group at church. She was with her family in Florida over Christmas, leaving him there alone with the kids.

Rob was a pro at hiding his pain. The years of arthritis made his tolerance increasingly high as the disease progressed. As the family gathered in Rob's family room, laughter filled the air as they shared their joy of the season together. Rob loved telling the kids stories about him and his brother Art, as they enjoyed adventures on the river. It was like a good Tom Sawyer tale, and Rob seemed to embellish the facts as they egged him on.

It wasn't long until the kids noticed the large present near the Christmas tree. Soon everyone was gathering next to it, as they lifted and examined the large wrapped present. They were all trying to guess what was in it. The package didn't say who it was for, only that it was from Santa. The tag said; "Merry Christmas, Santa." The kids were perplexed by it. Since it was from Santa, Rob's daughter wanted to ask him what it was, but couldn't because of the grandkids.

As Kate came into the room after preparing the side dishes for the meal, she told the kids that Rob helped Santa bring the present in last night, and she thought he might have told him what was in the box. The grandkids were begging Rob to tell them about the gift.

Rob smiled and said; "Santa made me promise not to tell."

Then Kate said, "Well, you will know soon enough because dinner is ready, and we will open the presents right after dinner."

Each year, they made it a tradition to order a large Honey Baked Ham. The meal was easy to prepare and didn't take long to assemble and serve. In addition to the large ham, were Kate's delicious scalloped potatoes, made from a recipe handed down from generation to generation. The bean casserole and a relish tray brought by Rob's daughter Laura completed the setting. The food was delicious, and they all delightfully stuffed themselves.

After dinner, the kids sorted the gifts by name, and then asked, "Who is the big one for?"

Rob smiled and said, "Santa told me it was for the two of you, but Santa also said, that it was to be shared with anyone in the family who wanted to use it."

"Can we open it?" they asked.

"Sure go ahead," Rob replied.

The box was hard to open and it seemed to take them forever to unwrap the festive paper that covered it. Rob decided to get a box cutter to cut the top of the box open to expedite the process.

When Rob cut the box open, the whole family laughed and said; "Santa should have labeled the gift to Papa."

Then Rob joined their laughter and said, "You're probably right, Santa knows what I like."

They all examined and touched the smooth basswood surface.

Rob's daughter said, "I suppose the cushioned seats are for the grandkids too."

After several minutes of jabbing and joking about Rob's love of tobogganing, they settled in to open the rest of the presents.

Rob had a special surprise for Kate when she opened her blanket. Sandwiched between the layers were airline tickets to Arizona. Kate and Rob dreamed about retiring there some day, and they tried to vacation there every winter. Rob had told her a couple of months earlier that he wanted to go somewhere different, and a vacation in Aspen to ski would be a perfect vacation. Rob knew the last thing Kate wanted to do was vacation in the snow. The setup was perfect and Kate bought it, "hook, line, and sinker."

Kate loved the warm weather, and unlike Rob, she didn't care much about playing in the snow. Rob really had her convinced that they were going to Colorado in February. The surprise of going to her favorite place on earth made her scream with joy. Then she went over and hit him on his sore arm, it was all Rob could do to keep from crying from the pain.

She said, "Are you okay?"

Rob played it cool and said, "Yes, I must have pulled a muscle."

Kate was so excited that she paid little attention to the excuse.

The grandkids also loved their new ice skates from Nana and Papa and they were excited because the town of Wheaton created an ice rink just off the town square. Rob taught the kids how to skate when they were about three years old, and as they grew, their proficiency made the activities great fun. Rob loved to skate rings around the kids and race them as he skated backwards. The years of him skating and playing hockey on the river with his brother made Rob quite the skater.

Rob joined the hockey team in college, but lacked the speed to make the varsity team. As he entered his junior year in college without making varsity, he lost interest and eventually dropped the sport. Rob never was very athletic like his older brother Art, who excelled at everything. In college, Art was on the varsity hockey team and was the school's leader in goals made. His athleticism made him very popular with the girls and that often made Rob feel somewhat inferior.

Art, although very smart, didn't take college seriously. He was only an average student. Rob, on the other hand, worked diligently to make all A's and graduated Summa Cum Laude. Their lives seemed to take on two different paths as they entered adulthood. But, in spite of Rob's lack of exceptional talent, he loved skating and even more than that, showing off in front of his grandkids.

The hours passed as the family enjoyed the festivities. Rob had everyone playing Wii games while he sat and watched. As they took turns playing, Kate wondered why Rob wasn't participating. The pain was numbed by a couple of glasses of wine, but Rob didn't want to aggravate the arm, so he didn't play.

As the family slowly said their good byes, Rob felt satisfied and content. He knew he was blessed to have such a close family. They all loved one another and loved spending time together. As the years passed, they all seemed to grow closer together.

Rob decided to give his arm some time to recover before he attempted to take on the steep toboggan hill. The snow fell all week, and as the week progressed, his arm seemed to get better. By the end of the week, he was anxious to finally get to the hill and try the new toboggan.

The following Saturday, early in the afternoon and Rob was excited to have his two grandchildren over to try out their new toboggan. The snow was fresh and the air crisp as they walked from the car to the steep forest preserve hill where the sledding was perfect. Rob's grandchildren were the perfect age for playing with Rob in the snow.

The tobogganing each year became the highlight of the winter. As the grandkids grew older, the pilgrimage with Rob became exciting and special. They loved how Rob would act like a little boy as he tried to scare them and increase the anticipation and danger by telling them stories of his adventures on the Fox River. Their grandfather, or Papa as they liked to call him, was that little boy at heart, making their adventures special.

Most years, by mid-December, they normally had plenty of snow to make some runs at the large hill. But this year, the icy surface conditions made it unsuitable for tobogganing. When Rob learned that the accumulation of snow would be over a foot, he couldn't wait to invite the grandkids over to play with him in the fresh snow. The kids loved coming over for the weekend of adventure and fun, but more than the fun, they loved their Papa and Nana.

The thought of tobogganing made Rob think about the great memories of him and his brother as they grew up on the river. Their home was perched on a steep hill that led down to the Fox River. The anticipation of snow and the river freezing over began in early November as the first signs of winter emerged. They would spend every spare moment traversing the hill and playing ice hockey when the deep freeze finally came.

Rob's brother, Art was two years older and was fearless. He often would challenge Rob with his dangerous paths that traversed through the trees and over ramps that they would build. Rob wasn't as daring as Art but he would never let on that he couldn't keep up with his older brother. The two of them were inseparable and this made their childhood exciting and filled with adventure and fun.

Rob could hardly wait for Saturday to come, because it made him feel young. Even though he was getting older, the boyish nature bonded him with his grandchildren. The kids would beg to come to Papa's house regardless of the occasion. Oh how Rob longed to be a boy again, free from the trials of life.

The drive from the house to the preserve took about twenty minutes and the discussion was centered on how fast the hill would be with the fresh snow. When they arrived, they took the new toboggan from the top of their old Suburban, and Rob waxed the bottom runners so they could go even faster. Rob was a pro at making the kids feel the rush of anticipated speed and danger, as they worked their way to the base of the run.

It was almost one-half mile to the base of the hill, and as they walked from the Suburban to the steep incline, Rob noticed that the pain was returning under his arm. He ignored his pain and continued as he rationalized what the cause of the pain was from. He wasn't how long he would be able to play given the pain that was gripping him now. Rob knew that he would eventually suffer with severe rheumatoid arthritis just as his mom had before she passed away. The last few years of increasing pain in his joints, made him realize that he was reaching an age that would limit his activities. The hill was groomed from the week of snow and from the other thrill seekers that were there from earlier in the day. Rob liked to go later in the day, so the snow would be packed by other toboggans for faster speeds.

A fresh light coating of new snow over the icy base would make it optimum for speed. As they climbed the hill to reach the summit, Rob could feel the ache intensify in his underarm. Even though he shrugged it off as old age, somehow he knew it was something different. As they reached the top, he asked the kids to sit for a few minutes to rest. As he sat there he realized that the pain wasn't getting better. He pulled himself onto the toboggan as he pushed it over the rise. The toboggan pulled them back, as it raced down the hill. Rob's pain was replaced by the adrenalin rush from the incredible speed. That was the fastest toboggan run that he had ever experienced, and the screams of joy from the kids enhanced his run down the steep hill.

The second climb to the top took Rob twice as long, and Rob asked the kids to help him carry the toboggan. Rob was now paralyzed with pain as they sat resting at the top of the hill. As they sat, the pain continued to increase, and it was all he could do to get on the toboggan and launch it down the hill.

At the bottom of the hill, the kids looked at Papa and could see that he was not his jovial self. He kept saying that he was fine, but the kids sensed that they should call it a day and head home. Rob finally realized that he would not be able to carry the toboggan back up the steep hill for another run. Rob's thoughts raced as he drove the 10 miles to his home in Wheaton. The joy of playing in the snow was replaced by the intense ache under his arm. Why was it so painful, he thought, and why was it now extended to his armpit?

When they arrived home, Kate was surprised they were home so soon. When she saw Rob, she knew something was wrong. Kate had a sixth sense for knowing exactly what was on Rob's mind and when he was in pain.

"What's wrong?" she asked.

He tried to act as if it was nothing, but she knew it was serious by his tone.

As he peeled off the layers of clothing, he could barely raise his arm. Every effort brought intense pain. The armpit was swollen and red. Rob wasn't able to extend his arm all the way up so Kate could examine it, but as he raised it to the point where she could see his underarm, a look of fright fell upon her face. Considering the look, he knew he was in trouble. After thirty eight years of marriage, he knew that look, and it scared him.

"Rob, you need to get to a hospital right away," Kate exclaimed.

She knew that his lymph nodes were extremely swollen and enflamed. It could be an infection, or worse than that cancer. Kate knew from her nursing experience that regardless, the condition was serious and needed a doctor's attention. As she thought about the fact that there would be no regular doctors available until Monday, she drove him to the hospital emergency room.

Fortunately, it was early enough that the normal Saturday night ER rush of injuries hadn't arrived. As they checked in, she was surprised by the lack of activity. The doctor was able to see him right away. After the standard checking of vital signs, Dr. Sam Reynolds did a thorough examination of the rest of his body. After ordering a number of blood tests, stat, he probed the other lymph areas and found that tenderness was present in several areas.

When the blood work came back, Kate knew from the doctor's face, the news wasn't good. She knew the moment she saw his condition that it was a serious problem. The doctor was calm and collected as he explained that he had elevated white blood cells, and the tests indicated high cell activity.

Diagnosis

Kate made some calls to the oncology doctor she had worked with at the hospital. He was regarded as the best in his field and was now doing research work at the university. His practice was limited to special cases, and Kate was hopeful that he would examine Rob as a favor. After several calls to colleagues and friends, she was able to contact him. As she explained Rob's condition, he agreed to see him first thing the next morning.

It was almost midnight by the time they had the testing done. Rob was sedated, and Kate decided that there wasn't anything else she could do, and Rob was fast asleep as a result of the pain killers. She figured that if she didn't get some sleep now, she would be sorry later. She told the nurse that she would be back early in the morning, and if Rob woke up to let him know that she went home to get some sleep and let the dog out.

The morning came quickly as Dr. Butler arrived to awaken Rob out of his deep sleep. Kate was already there and waiting in the room.

"Good morning doctor, may I have a word with you before you see my husband," Kate asked.

Dr. Butler was surprised when Kate asked him to leave the room. Kate was quivering as she told the doctor that she could see swollen lymph nodes on several areas of Rob's body, and that Rob was experiencing some pain from internal organs. The doctor thanked her for her observations and then returned to the room to examine Rob.

It didn't take him long to see that Rob had some major problems and needed a biopsy and a full MRI to determine the extent of his disease. The look on the doctor's face said it all as he tried to give Kate some encouraging words. We will need to see the results of various tests to see what we are dealing with and where we go from here. Kate knew that it would take a couple of days for the testing and subsequent results. As she sat looking at Rob, she could only wonder why God would allow him to go through this. She was thinking about all of the many memories shared with Rob over the past 35 years.

Rob was resting well as the pain medications were administered through an I.V. and the affects made him groggy. His eyes connected with Kate's and he knew that she was terrified.

"Kate," he said softly, "I know you're scared honey, but God is in control, and our real home is not here anyway."

Even though Kate knew Rob was right she couldn't stop the fear that she felt and the lack of control that gripped her. Rob took her hand and pulled her close kissing her cheek.

"I love you Kate, and I know that the years we have are numbered. I am so grateful that God has given me everything a man could hope for, a loving wife, a best friend, a purposeful life, a wonderful daughter and son in law and two beautiful grandchildren."

The word about Rob's hospital stay spread quickly and by the end of the day the hospital room was filled with family and friends. Pastor Dave came and prayed with Rob, along with some of the elders from their church family. Next came the notes, flowers, and the encouraging cards. Rob truly was loved by all and was being prayed for by many. The next two days seemed like an eternity as they waited for the prognosis.

Wednesday at 10:00 a.m. Dr. Butler arrived with the stack of reports and scans. The mood was somber, but positive, as he entered the room.

"Rob I'm afraid the news is not very good. In fact, there is no easy way for me to tell you this, but you have lymphatic cancer, stage five, and the pain you're experiencing is a result of the cancer spreading to the lymph nodes, the pancreas and liver. The MRI also revealed a tumor on you left lung and upper intestines."

Kate knew exactly what that meant and had to leave the room because she couldn't control her emotions.

After a few minutes of silence, Rob finally asked, "Is there any hope of recovery?"

The doctor trying to seem positive answered that in rare occasions, remission was possible, but treatment at this stage would be experimental, because his disease had spread too far and was beyond any conventional treatments.

He told him, "Rob, there are several new experimental procedures that, if you would like, could prolong your life. If you're interested I can discuss your condition and subsequent treatments with my associates. These treatments have very mixed results and by no means are proven in their effectiveness. Your accelerated condition qualifies you for treatments not available conventionally.

As the doctor was about to leave the room Rob asked, "How long do I have?"

The doctor answered, "Based upon the majority of cases that I have treated over the past twenty years as an Endocrinologist, three to six months, maybe longer."

Two Ways to an End

The doctor then said, "There is no way to accurately predict the progression of the disease, but sometimes the progression stalls and you could buy some additional time. I'm sorry Rob; I know that your wife will make the time you have left as comfortable as possible."

Kate entered the room and the doctor asked her if she was up to discussing how they would handle pain management.

"Yes," she said, "We need to know our options."

Kate overheard the conversation with Rob as she wept outside the room. Kate decided that she would take care of him herself and care for him at home. The doctor had explained that he was conducting clinical trials on terminal cancer patients, and Rob would qualify for the program if he was interested. So far, the results were very mixed, but in some of the cases, the treatment was effective.

She knew that Dr Butler was familiar with all the new cutting edge treatments, and the best chance of remission would be with those treatments. Kate asked the doctor if Rob could be cared for at home rather than in the hospital.

The doctor replied, "As long as you can get him into the lab once a week, we can treat him from home."

Kate was pleased that Rob would be able to go home, instead of having to stay in a sterile hospital room.

As the doctor reviewed the options for care and pain management, and Kate decided that she would take a leave of absence from work to care for Rob at home herself. Rob was wondering how the kids would handle the news and especially the grandkids. He also needed to discuss the situation with his company president. For the past twenty three years, Rob was the sales manager of a small insurance agency. His relationship with the owner and President was more like a partner than an employee. Rob knew that the likelihood of him working again was remote, and Stan, his boss, would need to assume his role until he could replace him. He also wondered if Stan would continue his salary for a few weeks or if Stan would release him right away.

Rob decided that he would ask Stan to meet with him at the hospital. When he called Stan he didn't let on about his condition. Stan agreed to meet with Rob knowing that it must be serious, if he wanted to meet at the hospital. Stan figured that Rob must need an operation and would need some time off. It never entered his mind that Rob would not be returning to his job. As Stan drove to the hospital, his thoughts turned to how much he cared about Rob, and that he would be missed even if were only for a short time.

Rob was thrifty and had saved a sizable amount of money over the years. In addition to his savings, Rob had contributed every year to his 401-K plan. Rob figured he had enough savings to last him through the illness. The thought of taking money out of his retirement fund didn't bother him because he had provided adequate life insurance for Kate in the event he passed away. Rob was on the final two years of paying off his mortgage, and he had been paying it down more rapidly over the past five years now that the kids were finished with college. It made Rob feel secure that Kate would be fine when he was gone.

When Stan arrived, he couldn't get over how many friends were there to visit Rob in the hospital. Stan hated hospitals and avoided them at all cost. He knew that if Rob wanted to meet there, it was only because he couldn't leave and needed to discuss something very important. Rob asked his other guests if they could give him a few minutes with Stan in private. Everyone understood and many told him that it was time for them to leave anyway. Rob hugged and said goodbye to all his friends as they left.

"Have a seat Stan," Rob said soberly, "I need to tell you what's going on here. I know I've kept you in the dark, but I wanted to examine my options before I talked with you."

"Stan, I'm afraid I won't be coming back to work. I have been diagnosed with terminal cancer and only have a few months to live."

Stan was in shock as Rob explained the details of the diagnosis. The thought of not having Rob at his company was overwhelming. As Stan looked at Rob he asked if there was anything that he could do to help. He knew Rob would be impossible to replace and the thought of not having him around, brought tears to his eyes. Stan was surprised at the feeling he had now that he knew Rob might not be back at work and gone from his life.

"Rob," he softly spoke, "I know your job is probably the last thing on your mind and your energy should be spent on your family and getting better. Please don't worry about your job, it will be open for you as long as you would like, and I'll continue your benefits to the end. I will take on your responsibilities until you return."

Rob knew Stan would have a tough time doing his job, and he would not be able to work at that pace for long. Stan asked Rob what he should tell his clients. Rob smiled because many of his clients were also friends.

"I feel like I need to call them personally," Rob said.

Stan was relieved that Rob would take the time to touch base with his clients and sales associates.

"I'll do it tomorrow Stan, the sooner the better. Stan, I just want you to know that the past twenty three years have been very fulfilling working for someone with your integrity and spiritual values. You've been a great friend."

Stan teared up as he listened and hugged Rob tightly as they said good bye.

"Don't give up buddy; I know you can lick this thing."

Stan put his thumb up and waved goodbye.

Kate came in and told Rob that he would be able to go home the next day after they did some blood work and series of x-rays. That was great news for Rob because he could be with his family and work on making some decisions going forward from the comfort of his home. They decided to just tell the grandkids that Papa was getting old and he needed rest. That way, they would understand when they saw him in bed. They figured that when the time came when they needed to explain his situation, they would limit the information and shield them from the trauma of the details.

When the other family members and friends came back to the room, Rob explained his condition. They all wept as he explained the extent of his disease. Rob tried to keep the conversation positive and upbeat, because he was privileged to receive a new cutting edge treatment. It was amazing how Rob was able to stay so composed and joyful. His courage was supernaturally received and was a model to everyone who was there.

They gathered around him and prayed that God would heal him. Kate asked the Lord to keep him comfortable and free from pain. She knew from the years of treating cancer patients that the disease was extremely painful. She also knew that as the disease progressed, Rob would need increased dosages of medications to manage the pain. She was thankful that Rob had a high tolerance for pain and that would help him through it.

Rob's family and friends said their good byes and left in shock over his prognosis. Many wondered why God would allow this trial, and if He would heal him. It was Rob's faith that comforted them as he told them not to be distraught because God was in control and that he was comfortable with whatever the outcome. His strength seemed to be unshakable as he smiled and hugged each one as they left.

Kate wanted to stay the night at the hospital, but Rob would not allow it. He told her that he would be home tomorrow and would have plenty of time to take care of him there.

He said, "It's more important for you to get rest."

He knew that Kate would wear herself out caring for him, and he didn't want her to get sick as a result of his illness. After some strong persuading, she finally yielded, and left for home.

The next morning, the papers came through for Rob's release from the hospital. Kate gathered all of Rob's belongings and put them in a gym bag she had brought.

Kate counted fifteen plants and flowers that were sent from friends and business associates. She knew that many of the patients never received any flowers and some were alone. The thirty three years of nursing intensified her sensitivity to the loneliness that so many patients experienced. She was often amazed at how many patients were left alone, as a result of broken family relationships. The reality of how cruel and selfish families could be when parents and loved ones were ill broke her heart.

She spent much of her free time, and off hours ministering to them. She brought tags from home and labeled them, "From God, You Are Loved," and then asked the head nurse who was a friend, if they would distribute the flowers to patients who weren't blessed with any flowers of their own. Kate would often pick up flowers from the local funeral home, and bring them to patients on her floor. The flowers always seemed to lift their spirit, and Kate used it as an opportunity to talk with them about God. The head nurse thought it was a great idea, and she agreed to take care of it.

Rob struggled, as he got out of bed and into the wheelchair. His pain was numbed by the painkillers, but he still needed help as he sat down in the chair. They wheeled him out, as he hugged a couple of the nurses that cared for him along the way. It was amazing how fast Rob could become friends with people and learn all about them. The ride home was quiet but positive, as Rob thanked Kate for making it possible to go home.

As they drove up to the house, Rob smiled and said, "It's so good to be home again, I've missed this place."

Kate had prepared their bedroom before hand, and she had pillows stacked to prop Rob up in the bed. That way, he could comfortably watch TV and eat. They both were thankful that his treatment could be done from home and that the grandkids could come and see him.

Relationships

The next day, Laura brought the grandkids over after school. They were so glad to see their Papa, and he also missed them. It had only been five days, but it seemed like much longer, and Rob loved the attention. The kids had made get well cards while he was in the hospital, and they presented them to him. His granddaughter drew pictures of them tobogganing that had big smiles on each of their faces as the toboggan raced down the steep hill. David, the grandson, drew them skating with all three of them hand-in-hand, as they went around the rink.

The kids climbed into bed with their Papa. They wanted to know what was wrong with him and why he was in bed. Rob explained, "Sometimes people get sick and eventually everyone gets old, and will die someday. God decides when our work here on earth is finished. Then God will take us to heaven, where there is no sickness. When we die, we are with Jesus, who has things for them to see and do in Heaven. Rob explained that he didn't know yet if that's what God wanted, but if God did want him to go there, they would someday see him again, because they too would eventually go there."

Rob's explanation prompted several questions from the kids.

"Papa," they asked, "why does God let people get sick?"

"That's a good question, Rob replied. It goes back to when God made the first man."

"You mean Adam?" Jen asked.

"Yes God made him perfect and Adam's wife Eve as well. God instructed Adam that if he ate the fruit from a forbidden tree in the center of the garden, he would die. Then they met this serpent, who lied to them, and got them to eat the fruit from the forbidden tree. God had no choice but to carry out his judgment, because they disobeyed Him. Much like when your mom tells you to do something and you disobey her, she then punishes you for not obeying. So God allowed the man and woman to age and as they aged, their bodies deteriorated. Eventually the body can't function, and they die."

Then Rob said; "The good news is that Jesus came to earth, and He is God's Son. He allowed Jesus to be killed on the cross, so that the payment of everyone's disobedience would be paid. That's why we believe in Him, and accept His gift to us, that pays for that punishment."

"So then what happens?" David asked.

"Well, when we die, we go to a place called Heaven. It's where God lives and it is wonderful. That's where my mom and dad are now. They are waiting for me to go there too, so they will be with me again." Rob replied.

Jen seemed to understand, but David seemed concerned and confused.

David took Rob's hand and asked him, "Are you going to die?"

Rob knew this was a complicated question for them and needed a careful reply.

He said, "David, that is not up to me to decide. God decides when that time is for each person. We will all go

there eventually and live forever. But in order to go to that special place, you must accept His gift and believe in Him. My time may come soon, or it may be much later. I will be happy either way, because I know that eventually we will all be together in Heaven,
and it is a place that is much more wonderful than you can imagine."

He went on to say, "Because we believe in Jesus, we don't have to worry about dying because we will live forever with God. If my body dies, I will get a new one that is much better because it can't get hurt and never gets sick or dies."

David seemed content with the explanation, and relieved that they would be together in heaven.

He then said, "I believe in Jesus, we learn about him in Sunday school, and He's in my heart."

Rob teared up as he looked at David's faith. How blessed he was to know that they both believed in the Lord.

The kids brought a board game to play. Hours seemed to fly by, as they played the game with him in bed. Kate could hear them laughing and Rob ribbing them, as they beat him easily at the game. As the early evening approached, Laura's husband Tim came over, and the whole family ate together in Rob's room.

Kate noticed that Rob was having a hard time with the standard king size bed, and the pillows didn't seem to support him very well. She decided that making him comfortable was more important than his room location, so they moved him into a spare bedroom that had a view of their picturesque back yard. A special bed was rented that allowed adjustments in various positions and helped manage his pain. The ability to change positions made his condition more tolerable.

The days seemed to fly by as Kate and Rob and his family spent more time together enjoying their close relationship, while laughing about their memories together. Kate took a leave of absence from work so she could be with Rob. Kate worked on putting together a portfolio of photos that they had collected over the years. She digitized the photos and organized them by date, location and occasion. She did this to pass the time as she sat with Rob every day. It was so much fun to examine each photo, and recall the fun times they enjoyed together. As they reviewed the photos, they came across some photos of the last reunion with his brother Art, just before their mom died.

It was over Christmas about seven years ago. Art had just divorced his third wife and was in Chicago on business. Rob was having the family over for Christmas Eve that year, because Christmas fell on a Sunday, and their church was having a candlelight church service. After an early dinner they opened presents and were enjoying the time together as a family. As the time came near to head off to church, Rob asked his brother if he could talk to him.

When Rob started to ask Art if he would to go with them to church, Art arrogantly announced that, he wasn't interested in going because, he didn't believe in God.

He looked irritated that Rob even asked, and said, "The Bible is just a bunch of fairy tales, and Christianity was for the weak."

There was no reasoning with him over the subject, and he left angry that Rob had even brought it up.

When their mom died two years later, Art made his appearance, but avoided any conversations about God. Both their mom and dad had made a decision to follow Christ. Rob was instrumental in their spiritual growth as they saw Rob change and devote himself to the faith. Rob kept asking them to go to church with them and after months of persistent requests, they began to go and receive the truth about Christianity. It was a year later when they finally turned to Jesus in faith at an altar call made by the pastor.

As the years went by, Rob's parents became very close to Rob and his family, and spent most of their free time together. Rob's mom died five years ago, and it was the first time in several years, where Art was present. When Rob recounted the family's spiritual journey at his mom's memorial service, Art became angry, walked out, and never came back. It was more than he could bear; hearing how close his brother was to them. The tensions became so bad that Art wouldn't even talk with Rob. Rob tried calling him repeatedly to reconcile their relationship, but Art wouldn't take or return his calls.

After Art moved to New York early in his career, he was thrust into the fast paced life that involved larger deals conducted by prominent leaders within the financial world. His views became very self serving as he mimicked their lifestyles. Rob and Art grew further and further apart, as Rob became what Art termed "religious."

Rob became a Christian when he was in his second year of college at Northwestern. The dorm room assigned by the school, paired him with a Christian roommate. His roommate's involvement in Campus Crusade for Christ was instrumental in Rob's lifestyle change. He persistently invited Rob to a Bible study at a local coffee shop. Rob reluctantly accepted after over a year of prodding. Within a few months of attending the Bible study and many discussions with his roommate, Rob gave his life to Christ.

Art was also a student at Northwestern. He was in his senior year, and didn't want anything to do with what he called "Jesus Freaks". Any conversations about God made him very uncomfortable. The reality of losing his brother as a party buddy, and the arguments over Rob's change to Christianity, made Art angry toward his younger brother. Art admitted that he was having too much fun to change his lifestyle, and it made it awkward for both of them. Art seemed to drift deeper and deeper into his self-absorbed pleasures. Dating numerous girls at once and it was all he talked about.

After graduation, Art decided that finding a position as a stockbroker would be the quickest path to wealth. Art took a position with Bear Sterns in Chicago. The opportunities seemed to be limitless, as Art moved up the ladder and finished his graduate work during the evenings. Art was driven and was too busy to enjoy life. He was on a mission to become a multi-millionaire by the age of thirty. By the time he reached the age of twenty-nine, Art had moved on as a partner in a small investment banking firm and had assets worth well over several million dollars.

Art married in his late twenties and had one daughter, Courtney. For a short time while Courtney was an infant, Art seemed to be more receptive to making his relationship with Rob and his parents better. Art hated the suburbs and would complain about having most of the family gatherings at Rob's house. Art loved the city and all the trappings of his fast paced lifestyle. As the years passed he seemed to become less interested in his wife and daughter and more involved at work. The relationship slowly deteriorated, as Art kept a girlfriend on the side, and would often be seen at social events with her.

As Art pursued his dreams, his quest for bigger deals consumed him. The deals became bigger, the stakes higher, and Art loved his increasing power. His reputation for putting deals together became known by the larger investment bankers in Manhattan. After eight years in Chicago, the temptation to become a partner with one of the leading investment bankers in New York became more than he could resist. The move to New York further aggravated a strained relationship with his wife and daughter, as Art was consumed with his work. He worked late every night putting together his deals. Art's wife finally left him within a year of moving to Manhattan. Art was consumed by the power and status that money could buy and was caught up in the world of wealth and power.

The road to riches and power was not without cost for Art. After his second and then third marriage, and a strained relationship with his only daughter, he finally admitted that his business was the only satisfaction that he had in life. His business deals came first and were all he could think and talk about. It seemed as though he didn't care at all about his daughter, and as the years passed, she finally stopped seeing or talking with him. Art lived an isolated life outside his business dealings. As the years passed, Art became addicted to alcohol and drugs and it slowly became more obvious to everyone around him.

Rob on the other hand, became a prolific student, and the time went fast as he finished his business degree at Northwestern. Rob took a job with a large insurance company in Chicago, and worked as a benefit administrator. After three years behind a desk, he made a decision to change his career path and took a job in sales for a small insurance agency in Elmhurst near his new home. Soon after, Rob met Stan at church. Stan owned a competing insurance agency and they immediately became close friends. For several years, Stan tried to get Rob to work for him. He finally accepted when Stan offered him a sales management position with the opportunity to substantially raise his income. Their relationship was great, as they built the agency together, and increased sales significantly over the years.

Rob met Kate in his senior year of college at a Campus Crusade retreat in Michigan. When Kate's brother, who was Rob's classmate, introduced them, it was love at first sight. Kate was a junior at the University of Chicago and had come to the retreat with her college roommate. Rob had dated several girls during college and was very popular. After his conversion to Christianity, he decided that finding someone with the same spiritual convictions and commitment to his faith was critical in deciding on a life partner. After learning that Kate was the section leader for Campus Crusade, Rob was convinced she was the one for him. The rest of the weekend was spent trying to sweep Kate off her feet. Kate liked Rob right away, but was tentative in the beginning, because she had just gotten over a three-year relationship that left her hurt and angry.

Kate reluctantly agreed to see Rob the following weekend. Rob couldn't wait to see her again, and it was all he could think of that week. Rob took Kate downtown to see Romeo and Juliet, which was playing at the Rush Street Theatre for a special showing. The theatre was packed, but the movie was perfect to set their romance in motion. They spent the next month together, working around their busy schedules. As the days went by, they decided that their studies were suffering and that they should only get together on the weekends. If was only four months into their dating, when Rob asked Kate to marry him. Kate knew that Rob was the one for her and without hesitation accepted his proposal.

The following September, they wed at Kate's home Church in Elmhurst. The reception was beautiful, and the entire family thought that they were a perfect match for one another. After their marriage, they made the decision to live downtown close to the University so Kate could finish her senior year in college, and Rob would be close to his employer. The next three years went quickly as Kate graduated from college and took a nursing job at Northwestern Medical Center. Rob continued his work at the Insurance

Company, but he really didn't like his job.

Rob was determined to move closer to their family, and so they saved every spare dollar for three years to buy a small house in the western suburb of Wheaton. The small two bedroom house was perfect for them. The neighborhood was great with a mixture of small and larger homes on larger lots. The older neighborhood was inviting, and Rob and Kate soon gained many friends on their block. After they bought the house, they made job changes to bring them closer to their home. Kate was pregnant with their first child, and the support of her family would make juggling a nursing job while raising children much easier.

Kate gave birth to a beautiful baby girl, and then two years later was pregnant with another child. When they learned about her second pregnancy, they decided to put an addition on their cozy little home. The additional two bedrooms and a great room made the home perfect for their growing family. Rob wanted to have a son in the worst way, but Kate's second pregnancy was problematic and the boy Rob wanted so badly was still born. The complications left her unable to have additional children. Rob was angry with God for a long time, but as the years passed, he seemed to heal.

Raising their daughter, Laura, was a delight and time seemed to fly by. Rob would take her fishing, hiking and camping, trying his best to turn her into a little boy. Laura was feminine and sweet and as she grew older, it was obvious that his attempt to make her the son he never had was futile. Rob would often imagine what it would be like to have a son that he could take on adventures. The void of not having a son seemed to disappear when Rob became a grandfather.

Their life was filled with purpose, as they got involved in mentoring young married couples at church. Rob's teaching abilities, along with his charismatic personality, kept him very busy. As the years went by, it seemed like everyone at Wheaton Bible Church knew them and life was great. Laura was involved in youth ministry, and her faith in God grew stronger as she approached adulthood. Her life revolved around her relationship with God, and was a testimony to everyone who came into contact with her. It was a joy for Rob and Kate to watch her mature and grow in her faith.

Eventually Laura married the youth pastor at their Church. It wasn't long after Laura's marriage that they would start their own family. Laura gave birth to a beautiful girl, and two years later gave birth to a perfect little boy. The two grandchildren were the joy of Rob's life, they made his life complete. His relationship with each of them made him realize how blessed he truly was, and he was very grateful.

Passing

"Even though I walk through the valley of the shadow of death, I will fear no evil, for you are with me; your rod and your staff, they comfort me." Psalm 23:4

A month had passed, and Rob was getting weaker as his disease progressed. The treatments were not working, and the cancer was spreading rapidly. Rob tried to ignore the intense pain, but the increasing need to take higher doses of pain killers made him sleepy and drained most of the time. When the family came over to visit, it would be for shorter periods, as Kate limited their stays.

The grandkids could tell Rob was not getting better, and they often questioned why they couldn't spend more time playing with him. Rob tried to act as if he was going to be fine, but the pain made it very difficult to keep his jovial demeanor. Rob tried to make the visits less frequent to slowly prepare them for his departure. He didn't want the kids to feel traumatized over his eventual departure.

The pastor would come each week to pray over Rob. He was convinced that Rob would go into total remission, and the miracle would be a testimony to the power of God. Rob could tell that the treatments and the prayers for whatever reason were not working. He accepted the outcome and made a point of remaining positive with his outlook. Rob considered making an appearance before the congregation to tell them that he was looking forward to actually meeting Jesus and being before the throne of God. He realized that he couldn't muster enough energy to make it there, so he wrote them a letter thanking them for all their prayers.

There were so many people praying for Rob, it was amazing. Kate and Laura created a web site with a blog so everyone could get updates of his condition. Rob would often have Kate video tape himself, as he gave them some encouraging words. He would thank them for their prayers, and as time passed, he knew God was hearing them because he felt at peace with his condition. Rob liked reading the blog, and the grandkids always wrote to Rob before they went to bed, letting him know how much they loved and missed him. The kids were so sweet; Rob knew that they would miss each other and Rob would miss watching them grow.

Even though Rob was in pain and suffering, he never seemed to get him down. He would say, "The Lord has His reasons for my condition that is beyond what we can see." His faith and optimism was a testimony to someone who closeness to God was visible through him. As people came to visit Rob, they always seemed to leave in a better frame of mind than when they had come. His positive outlook made everyone feel comfortable and glad that they came to see him. It was amazing how many friends he had and how each of them seemed to have a special connection with him.

As time passed, the thoughts of his brother and their strained relationship kept haunting him. Over the years their relationship disintegrated and left them at odds. Ever since Rob started going to Church, their paths seemed to take opposite directions. After college, Art would avoid family get togethers because he was too busy with his work and going to school at night. Art's pursuit of money and power consumed him and made everyone uncomfortable when he was around. Their mom would always make excuses for Art, as his life went into high gear financially, and he was never around.

The money seemed to feed on his ego, and make him unapproachable. The more successful he became the more arrogant and unapproachable he became. His desire to be the center of attention repelled everyone who was around him. Art didn't seem to care who he hurt, as long as he got what he wanted. Most of the people who spent time with Art had ulterior motives. Many would try to take advantage of his success. Everything Art touched seemed to turn to gold.

His reputation was legendary, as he climbed the ladder of success. After he finished his graduate work and received his MBA, the opportunities seemed to rapidly increase. The offers were limitless, and the successes many, as he progressed and became wealthy.

When Art finally did make it to a family get together, it was only for a few minutes, and then it was as if he couldn't wait to leave. Occasionally, he would bring a new girlfriend or new wife around, only to show off his ability to attract gorgeous women. Even his marriages were set up and centered in exotic locations, where he could mix business with pleasure. The family, although they were invited, never seemed included. Art liked having several intimate relationships going at the same time. It was if he wanted to see how many lives he could control and manipulate at once. The relationships always seemed to end badly, and his ex-wives seemed to hate him.

Every time Rob tried to reach out to his brother, it seemed to end in an argument. Rob knew how misguided Art was, and that all the power, money or accomplishments would never satisfy him. He kept thinking back to the conversation that they had at their mom's funeral, where Art bluntly proclaimed that, "he didn't believe in God, and the thought of heaven or hell was a bunch of bunk." His philosophy was, "live for today, try to get whatever you can, and forget about who gets in the way." This also seemed to be the view most of his associates. It made it difficult to talk to him. Rob knew that Art was headed for hell, and didn't know how to prevent it. The reality of the brevity of his own life gripped him, as he knew that time was running out quickly.

Rob asked Kate what she thought he should do.

Kate said, "Why don't you write him a letter. Fill it with memories from your childhood, and tell him how much you care about him. Express how you feel as he enters his later years and that rejecting the need for a Savior grieves you."

A tear welled up thinking about how he wanted to let him know how he felt. Then he looked into Kate's eyes and said, "You are so wise, what would I ever do without you. I'll start writing it today."

Kate seemed to have a special giftedness and wisdom when it involved how to handle a given situation. Her insight often steered Rob to make good decisions. She could see things from the other person's perspective. Rob was excited about writing the letter because it would give him a greater purpose that would take his focus off his illness. As time went by, it seemed to be the highlight of his day.

When Kate had called Art to tell him about his brother's cancer, he seemed to get choked up and said that he was truly sorry. He said that he would try to schedule a trip in the Chicago area over the next couple of months, so he could visit Rob. Three months had passed, and they hadn't heard back from him. The reality of Art visiting Rob was remote at best, and even if he did visit, it most likely would be a short appearance so Art wouldn't feel guilty. Art had asked Kate if he could do anything to help. Kate knew it was just a courtesy and that he was just trying to console her.

She said, "Art, if you can't come out and see Rob, at least pick up the phone and call him. Rob really misses you." Art was silent and finally said, "I've got another call coming in, and so I'll talk with you later." Then he hung up, before she could say anything.

Art sat thinking about his brother, as a rush of emotion fell over him. The reality of death gripped him, as he thought about him being older than Rob. He was beginning to feel the effects of getting old himself. After a few minutes he thought, I can't think about such things and besides I'm in great shape. He realized that it had been a year since he had a physical, and he had better go in and get checked out as a precaution. Art still played on a hockey league and worked out while watching CNN every morning. He prided himself in having a toned body, and he worked hard at keeping it perfect.

Rob worked on writing the letter to Art for several weeks. The effects of the medication to control his increasing pain made it impossible to work on it for any extended length of time. Rob's experimental treatments didn't seem to help at all, and it was evident to all that Rob wouldn't be around much longer. Rob would try to spend at least a few minutes each day writing his letter. He knew this was the only chance he would have to share the burden of his heart with Art. Rob crafted the words carefully and as the joyous boyhood memories raced through his mind, he realized how much he had loved his brother growing up. After seven weeks, he finally finished the letter and asked Kate if she would drop it in the mail.

Kate asked Rob if she could read the letter before she mailed it. Rob agreed, and then said, that he would be honored if she would. He wanted to know if she thought it would be effective in reaching his hardened heart. His prayer was that it would make Art think about the brevity of his life. As Kate read the letter that evening, she began to weep. Rob had such a big heart, and it was so evident in the letter. She prayed that the letter would reach Art's heart and make him realize the truly important things in life. The letter touched her so dramatically that she decided to make a copy for herself. She knew it would be something to remember Rob by. Kate fell to her knees and prayed that the Lord would use the letter in reaching Art and restoring their relationship. She then sealed it and dropped it in the mailbox later that evening.

The next morning she looked in on Rob, she could tell he was deteriorating quickly and that he was in bad shape.

"Why didn't you wake me?" she asked.

Rob was very weak and needed help to get to the bathroom. The pain was excruciating and at times, it took his breath away. The medications that he was taking were not taking the pain away, and Kate knew she needed to get him to the hospital. She called an ambulance and then called the family to let them know the situation. It was wonderful that the grandkids were able to see him that weekend. Rob seemed to have had a rush of energy, as he had played games with them. Rob knew his time was now short, and he wanted the pain to end. He prayed that the Lord would take him quickly, without an extended time of suffering.

As they pulled into the hospital, Rob asked if she had gotten the letter off.

"I just mailed it last night. Art should get it tomorrow," she said.

"Rob, the letter was wonderful. I spent some time praying over it, and asked that the Lord would use it to reach Art. It was very powerful and heart warming. Your love came out throughout the letter. I pray he will receive it with an open heart and mind."

Rob softly said, "I am so thankful that the Lord granted me enough time to finish it. I believe the pain from my illness helped me write it from a more loving perspective. I know God's ways are not mine, and if this sickness was the only way for me to reach Art, then it was well worth it."

Kate welled up with tears and said, "You are such a good man, and I am so thankful to have you as my soul mate."

Rob pulled her hand in and kissed it.

"No Kate," he said, "it's you who makes me who I am. The letter was your idea, and God took it from there."

"Kate, I'm going to miss you and the kids. My only comfort is that you will all be joining me there some day. What a great comfort to know where you're going when you die. I can't imagine what it would be like to go through this and not know that. How awful it is that so many people do not have that assurance."

Kate wondered what heaven would be like, and as she looked down at Rob, she thought about what the Bible says; "there will be no more pain, no more suffering; every tear will be wiped away." She realized how much better it would be when Rob didn't have the pain any more. She wished she could take it away herself. If she wanted it gone, she thought how much more the Heavenly Father would also want it gone. Kate knew Rob was at his end, and she prayed that he would go quickly and peacefully.

After several phone calls, Kate finally reached Dr. Butler as they wheeled Rob into the hospital ER. After examining Rob, the resident doctor made the decision to put Rob in intensive care. After Rob was situated in the room, they allowed Kate to go into the room. Dr. Butler came shortly after, and after examining Rob, he asked him if he could handle the pain. The Doctor knew that Rob was feeling pain everywhere and that it must be all he could do but to cry out. Rob softly said, "No more pain killers, I want to say goodbye to my family and more morphine will knock me out." The doctor was amazed at Rob's strength and unselfishness, and told Kate that Rob probably wouldn't make it through the day.

Rob was getting weaker and weaker, and it was all he could do to say, "Thank you Kate for caring for me."

About an hour later, the entire family came and were waiting to see Rob. As the family came in, Rob opened his eyes and asked the family to gather around him. Rob told the family that he was ready to go home and be with the Lord. He told them that he couldn't ask for a better family and that his life was the best. He then kissed them one by one, and as Kate kissed and hugged him, he closed his eyes and within a few minutes was gone.

Rob had a smile on his face as he went to be with the Lord. It was as if he saw heaven's gate open for him. The family gathered around him and prayed one by one. A peace fell over them, and they were glad that Rob's pain was gone and that he was now in a better place. They were sad only because they would miss him, and his loss would leave a void in each of their lives.

Heavens Gate

In a twinkling of an eye, Rob was escorted by angels and was standing in front of an enormous entrance to a city. The beauty of it was beyond description and for a moment, it took Rob's breath away. He was in awe. Before him, was a massive city set on translucent stones. The base dazzled with vibrant colors as the light from inside the city reflected in various patterns. It was the most spectacular sight he had ever seen, beyond anything he could have ever imagined.

As he stood there trying to take it all in, he thought how the description he had read in the Bible of Heaven, could never accurately describe what he was now seeing. The stones, although separate, were set perfectly together in a way that intensified their brilliance. Facets of light in pure spectral colors surrounded the glowing foundation. The colors were intense, yet soothing to the eye.

The city was vast. Rob looked upward and then to each side. He couldn't see where the city ended. Rob had seen many beautiful things on earth, but they were nothing in comparison to what he was taking in as he stood in wonder. The sight was something he never could have dreamed or imagined. The walls of the city were pure jasper, transparent and brilliant. The light pierced through the walls and made the entire city sparkle with light.

The foundation of the city was built on twelve layers of precious stones set in perfect order to maximize their color and brilliance. The layers of stone were inlaid with contrasting faceted stones in a variety of shapes and sizes. The first layer was jasper; the second sapphires; the third chalcedony; the fourth emerald; the fifth sardonyx; the sixth sarddus; the seventh chrysolite; the eighth beryl; the ninth topaz; the tenth chrysoprase; the eleventh jacinth; and the twelfth amethyst.

The gate was a large pearl that glistened and looked magnificent. Its enormous size almost looked immovable. The large pearl gate had a beautiful iridescent look that seemed to change, as soft hues reflected and bounced off the surface from the foundation stones. A frame was made of pure translucent gold and surrounded the enormous pearl. The gold frame was fashioned with ornate symbols and enhancements. At the top was inscribed one of the twelve tribes of Israel, made from insets of precious gemstones. Each gate had one of the twelve tribes of Israel fashioned in stone like the foundation. On the foundations were the names each of the twelve apostles inset with contrasting precious stones cut to fashion the name of each.

The gate was open and there was an immovable angel standing in front of the entrance as a sentry. The angel looked radiant and powerful. He glowed with energy unlike anything Rob had ever seen. Rob was afraid to look at him in fear. Another angel appeared at the gate and he was holding a large book bound in fine leather with precious gems inlaid in the cover. The angels were massive and adorned in armor made of various metallic colors.

The angel with the book summoned Rob to come to him. As Rob approached the angel, he asked him his name.

Rob answered, "Robert Bakken."

He opened the book and found his name written in the book and immediately the angel stepped to one side, smiled, and said; you may enter. The two sentries moved aside from the open gate as the brilliant light from inside the city cascaded from the entrance.

As Rob moved forward through the massive entrance, the light from within the city penetrated the surface that Rob was walking on. The surface was a transparent form of pure gold. The reflections made everything even more intensified and glorious. How wonderful it was to be here and experience the wonder of God in his infinite creation. Everything inside the city was transparent allowing Gods glory to penetrate through it.

When Rob made it through the thick threshold, he could see the radiant light which was illuminating the city was approaching the entrance. As the light approached, rays of spectral color danced on the entire city as if everything in the city were alive. The light, although intense, was not blinding but rather soothing. It was pure and radiant and penetrated everything in its path. As the light came nearer to Rob, he realized it was Jesus standing there to welcome him. Rob immediately knew it was Jesus because he could feel pure joy entering him as he approached.

Rob fell down before Him and was shaking uncontrollably.

Jesus put His hand on his shoulder and said, "Fear not, arise."

Rob felt a peace flow through his whole body the moment He touched him; it was the most wonderful feeling he had ever experienced.

Jesus dazzled with the glow of His glory. He was like a bolt of lightning, pure and brilliant. His hair and face were a radiant white that glowed. His eyes were like intense lasers burning like fire and penetrated everything around

Him. His body was physical but in a way Rob never expected. It was as if He had another dimension that radiated with His movement. Rob could feel the intense power that poured out of Him.

Jesus was dressed in a white robe with a golden sash around His chest. He was set aglow from the glory of his body underneath it. Rob looked down and saw His feet. They were like burnished bronze glowing in a furnace. As Jesus touched Rob he could see the nail scares on His hands. His presence was powerful and shook the air around him. His presence was intense but soothing at the same time. His voice wasn't audible but rather spiritual. It was like the sound of rushing waters; powerful and mighty, like the roar of a lion. He was unmistakably God Almighty in voice and presence. He couldn't believe he was actually standing there before his Lord.

Rob fell down before Him in awe once again.

Jesus then said powerfully; "I am the Alpha and the Omega, who is, and who was, and is to come, the Almighty. I am the Living One; I was dead, and behold I am alive for ever and ever! And I hold the keys to death and Hades."

"Rise and be cleansed," Jesus commanded.

Jesus was speaking to him through thought, not sound. Rob couldn't believe how incredible it was to experience this pure form of communication.

Jesus smiled and said, "Rob, you were bound by your old flesh. Expression and thought can now be received without the limitations of speech and sound. Pure thought expresses the heart perfectly and has no barriers. You are no longer bound by your flesh so the need to hear sound is now communicated Spirit to spirit."

As Rob stood up, Jesus looked into Rob's eyes, and suddenly Rob's entire life seemed to play before him in an instant. The good things, the bad things, and the unspeakable things, that were held in his heart. Jesus penetrated Rob's inner soul, suddenly, his sin and all that was impure, was burned away before his very eyes. The joy permeated him, as the dark things in his life were obliterated leaving only the pure acts of obedience and service to the Lord playing before him throughout his entire life. Rob began to fill with pure joy, as he saw the deceit and evil dissipate and leave him. Jesus held him up and smiled, as He pulled him into His bosom.

Jesus then placed his hands on both of Rob's shoulders as He faced him and said, well done good and faithful servant, great is your reward." Jesus handed Rob a white stone and on it was a name that Jesus gave to him that expressed His love for him. Rob looked at it and held it against his heart and said. "Lord I don't deserve this name! I am so humbled by your generosity toward me! You are pure Love!"

An angel then approached holding a crown adorned with brilliant gems and transparent gold.

Jesus placed the crown on Rob's head and said, "This is your crown of life Rob, come into Our city."

Jesus led Rob down the golden street into the Holy city. The joy that Rob was experiencing was so incredible, he couldn't speak. Jesus smiled and was pleased to see the thrill that was evident on Rob's face.

As they were walking, Rob became aware that he too had some form of a body. It was him, but translucent and shimmering a better representation of himself. It was perfect in every way. The structure was familiar but enhanced and made him feel exuberant. There was no pain and every move and every sensation felt wonderful. The body was not flesh but still had a substance to it.

The infilling of pure energy raced through his new body, and he felt as if he could do anything that he could imagine. The thought of physically maneuvering in any way he would like made the experience blissful.

Jesus said to him as they were walking, "Are you surprised at your soul body?"

Rob seemed perplexed, and replied, "Soul body?"

"Yes," Jesus said, "You've always had it, but on earth the soul is not visible as it is here. Your soul was your inner spiritual shell that is now out of your physical earthly body. Your soul body is much like the angels, who are spirit beings. You will come to understand better when you see others who are here."

As Jesus led him along toward another light that was far away illuminating the Holy City, he felt like a bride walking down the isle to be married. The rush of emotions were absent of sorrow, and everything was taken in and treasured. Every step revealed even more spectacular sights. The city was enormous with mansions in architectural styles he had never seen before.

He was only a few steps into the walk when they approached a woman standing with her arms out to hug Rob. He could hardly believe his eyes, because it was his mom. Although she was ageless in her appearance, she looked like he remembered her when he was a young boy.

Then his dad approached him and gave him a huge hug as he laughed with joy. Rob's emotions were stronger than he could ever remember. It was similar to the feeling he had when Kate gave birth to their daughter Laura. As they hugged each other, Rob was taken back by the sensation of touch as they embraced. It was so pleasurable and intimate; Rob didn't want it to end. Rob's mom told him that they have been excited knowing that he was going to join them. Their reunion was all they could talk about.

Rob's dad said, "This is just the beginning, each day brings wonders that are beyond description. You never get use to it."

"If what I've seen so far was all that there was, it would be so much more than I could have ever imagined. I've only been here a few minutes, and I'm already overwhelmed. You mean it gets better?" Rob asked.

"Yes Rob it does," his dad replied, "you haven't seen the Father yet."

"The best part of it all," his mom exclaimed, "is that we will experience this for eternity."

"The time seems to fly by," Rob's dad proclaimed, "as you learn about God and His mysteries."

Rob stood back from his parents so he could have a good look at them.

"I can't get over how young you are!" he said.

Rob's dad then said, "Yes Rob, here our bodies are better than the best athlete back on earth. The best part is that it doesn't wear out or get old. Each day when I look at myself, I think, how blessed I am to be here. You will learn that you are capable of feats that are staggering in terms of our old bodies. The best part is, you can't hurt them, and they are indestructible."

As Rob examined them, he realized that their appearance and composition was so different. Their skin was radiant and beamed with an energy that made them look attractive in spite of their imperfect features. Rob's father had a large nose with a lump in the center of it, but even that, unattractive back on earth, seemed attractive now. Rob wondered how he would look to himself. As he looked down at his hands he could see that they were a perfected form of himself with an increased energy. Their surface had a radiated glow that felt an enhanced sensation with any sort of contact. The sensation of well being and fulfillment was indescribable.

The last time he had seen his mom alive, she was in a wheelchair, crippled from her arthritis. To see her in her perfection was pure joy to Rob's heart. Her pain and suffering was replaced with a body that glowed with energy. She seemed to know what he was thinking as he looked at her.

"Rob," she said; "Guess what else? These bodies aren't even the final models we will receive."

Rob looked puzzled, "What do you mean?" Rob asked.

She pointed to Jesus and said, "When the resurrection occurs, we will receive glorified bodies like Jesus."

Rob seemed surprised, "your kidding!" he exclaimed.

"No Rob," Jesus interjected, "you will have the ability to travel in time and space without limits just as I do."

Rob thought to himself, how fun it would be to test his body to see what he could do. He asked his father if they could get together later so he could show him the new capabilities of his new body.

Rob's dad said, "Sure, but you will be busy learning about Heaven and the wonders of the Lord. You will be with Jesus for some time, and you will learn soon enough that for the most part, you can do whatever your mind conceives it to do."

"Come with me Rob," Jesus said, "I want you to see some of what I have been preparing for you. Then best of all, you will see the Father."

Jesus took Rob to what seemed to him to be the central part of the city. From the center to as far as Rob could see, there flowed a beautiful river. The river had trees lining it that were perfect in size, shape and appearance.

The trees had fantastic fruits on each of them. Some of the people were picking the fruit, while others were eating the fruit. The river was glassy blue, as the water shimmered and contrasted with the golden street. The river flowed from the center where the Father's throne was aglow. Flowers of every imaginable color and variety surrounded the landscape. Golden walkways meandered everywhere. Light bounced off the landscape, as the golden streets and translucent stones made everything more vivid with color. The intensity of color and radiant glow from the Glory of God looked magical.

Then Rob saw a beautiful golden trellis that led into a magnificent garden. The trellis had blossoms growing in a pattern at the top that read, Eden. Two massive angels were at its entrance similar to the entrance into the Holy City. They were guarding the entry where two other angels with trumpets that announced the entry of each individual as they passed through the gate. Rob looked surprised as they walked up to the archway and the angels sounded their trumpets and shouted, "Rob Bakken."

The garden was magnificent with color so vivid; it took his breath away. There were other people pruning and manicuring the lush plants.

"Rob," Jesus said, "Are you surprised that there are people here working in the garden?"

Rob was surprised and shook his head as he took it in.

Jesus explained that the people attending the garden do so because they love the garden. Their creativity is expressed in the colors, patterns, and beautiful setting that they conceive. It's what brings them pleasure and joy. I often walk with each of them, as they show me their wonderful creations. Rob couldn't get over how everything in the garden was perfect, and how the plants looked so much different than they did on earth.

Jesus knew what Rob was thinking and said, "You're probably wondering why everything looks so different here."

Rob nodded to affirm him, as he looked all about in wonderment.

The conditions here are different Rob, the life and illumination of all things comes from the glory of the Father. His glory is a life source that is incomprehensible and infinite.

Rob was soaking up the radiance of God's glory when suddenly he realized that even his own body was glowing from the glory of God. He felt such a wonderful energy, it was indescribable. Jesus smiled as he plucked one of the bright blossoms from a large plant. Instantly, the blossom was replaced and restored. The blossom that Jesus held twinkled and seemed attached to him as if it were an extension of his body. Rob was amazed as he looked closely at the blossom. He seemed to be able to see through it, as if he had some sort of super natural vision.

"Rob," Jesus said, "Your senses here are not limited to the physical. You are a spirit being, and you are without the limitations of the flesh that you had on earth. Because your senses are heightened, everything that you experience and see is intensified. You will never find your experiences here to be normal, because your senses are intensified within you, from the glory that fills the space. The Father has made joy complete in every way."

Rob didn't fully understand what this all meant, but he did know that regardless of his limited understanding, it was wonderful beyond description.

Jesus led him through waterfalls and crystal formations that kept getting more and more spectacular as they traveled through the garden.

As they walked, Rob said, "I can see why so many people come here to tend the garden, it's so beautiful, and I feel so fulfilled here."

Jesus then said, "This is what it was originally like on earth when we created Adam and Eve."

"Adam and Eve didn't realize what they had until We removed them from Our presence. It was too late to reverse their poor choice. The deceiver, Satan, is not allowed access to the garden any longer. That's why you saw cherubim at the entrance. Not only was Adam and Eve denied access into the garden, but Satan was banned as well. Now he has no access in the heavens, and only limited access directly before the Father's throne. Soon, he will be banished from here entirely and cast into the lake of fire forever."

Rob wondered why there were no children there. He wondered if Jason, their still born child would be there. His death devastated them back on earth and was a sorrowful time for the whole family.

Jesus knew what was on Rob's mind and suddenly before him was a man that Rob didn't recognize. He came up to Rob with a huge smile, and hugged him. As he did so, Rob immediately knew it was his son Jason. Rob laughed and said, "You're not a child!"

Jason smiled and said, "We do not have physical bodies here Dad, and our souls do not have a physical age."

Jesus then explained that when a soul and spirit are taken from the body, it becomes ageless, because your spirit does not die. When the flesh is removed what remains is your soul. When a child dies, knowledge is imputed through their relationship with Us as soon as they arrive in Heaven. The sin and separation that exists in the flesh which separates mankind from God, has been eliminated. Their souls are enlightened with knowledge and never experience the pain that sin produces.

"Rob," Jesus said, "They are the fortunate ones, because they did not have to endure the evil of the world, and the lusts of their flesh, which separate relationship and access to Us."

Rob was so excited about seeing Jason and the reality of what was just revealed to him. He started leaping with joy.

Rob looked at Jesus and said, "The mystery of what happens to children and the unborn, haunted me my whole adult life. I am so ashamed that I couldn't see, nor had the faith and trust that you would provide for them and have a special place for them here."

Although Rob knew intellectually that God is love, he needed to see it for himself to fully understand His infinite, boundless love.

Rob looked at Jason and said, "You and I have a lot of catching up to do."

Jason smiled and said, "I've spent a lot of time with my grandparents over the past five years, and they've told me all the stories about you. I can't wait to spend more time together and enjoy learning about you and the family. I am so blessed to have you as a dad, thank you."

Jesus looked at them and said to Jason, "We will see you later at the banquet."

Rob seemed confused and asked, "What banquet?"

Jesus smiled and said, "It's a surprise, you will know soon enough."

Rob hugged Jason again, and then instantly, he was gone.

"This garden leads to the Father's throne," Jesus explained. "I know that you will want to experience time before Him before you continue your tour. What you are seeing here is nothing compared to what's in store for you as we approach the throne of the Father."

As they moved toward the end of the garden, the light from the Father's throne intensified, drawing Rob toward it. Faint music so beautiful and glorious softly filled the air. Rob sensed the best was yet to come.

The Throne of God

As they moved toward the center of the city away from the garden, Rob could hear the beautiful music intensify and become more glorious. The choruses were unlike anything he had ever heard. The sound was pure and had a resonance that was unique and glorious. As they exited the garden, God's throne became visible. The Glory of God pulled Rob toward him and took his breath away.

At the very center, Rob could see a light so bright, it was difficult to look at it directly. The radiance and beams of God's glory flowed from his throne. On the throne was an indistinct form that seemed to change continually. It was a form of pure light, that was indescribable. As Rob approached the light, he could feel in the center of his soul, the pure love that flowed from God the Father. Rob suddenly had a new supernatural knowledge; that through him, and in him, is everything that is good. His awareness of how incredibly Holy God is, and how insignificant he was compared to him, made him fall down on his face before Him.

The Lord glowed like burning bronze and spectrums of light surrounded him, creating a rainbow above Him, vibrant with color and beautiful beyond description. In front of His radiance were four angelic creatures, resonant with life. They each had four faces and four wings. Their legs were as sturdy and straight as columns, but their feet were hoofed like those of a calf and sparkled like burnished bronze. On all four sides under their wings they had human hands. All four had both faces and wings, with the wings, touching one another. They turned neither one way nor the other; they went straight forward. They were cherubim created to worship God.

Their faces looked like this: In front a human face, on the right side the face of a lion, on the left the face of an ox, and in back the face of an eagle. Their wings were spread out with the tips of one pair touching the angel on either side. The other pair of wings covered their bodies. Each of them moved straight ahead. Wherever the spirit went, they went. They didn't turn as they moved. They appeared like a blazing fire. Tongues of fire shot back and forth between them, and out of the fire came bolts of lightning. The cherubim flashed back and forth like strikes of lightning.

As Rob watched the four cherubim, he saw something that looked like a wheel on the ground beside each of them. The wheels looked like they were identical, sparkling like diamonds in the sun. It looked as if they were wheels within wheels, like a gyroscope.

They moved in any one of the four directions they faced, but straight, not veering off. The rims were immense, circled with eyes. When the living creatures went, the wheels went; when the living creatures lifted off, the wheels lifted off. Wherever the spirit went, they went, the wheels sticking right with them, for the spirit of the living creatures were in the wheels.

Over the heads of the cherubim was something like a dome, shimmering like a sky full of cut glass, vaulted over their heads. Under the dome, one set of wings was extended toward the others, with another set of wings covering their bodies. When they moved Rob heard their wings, it was like the roar of a great waterfall, like the voice of God, like the noise of a battlefield. When they stopped, they folded their wings.

And then, as they stood with folded wings, there was a voice from above the dome over their heads. Above the dome there was what looked like a throne, sky-blue like a sapphire, with a humanlike figure towering above the throne. Rob could see from the waist up, he looked like burnished bronze and from the waist down like a blazing fire. Brightness was everywhere! The way a rainbow springs out of the sky on a rainy day—that's what it was like. It was the Glory of God!

The four creatures looked like a blazing fire or like fiery torches. Tongues of fire shot back and forth between the creatures and out of the fire, bolts of lightning. The creatures flashed back and forth like strikes of lightning.

When Rob saw all this, he fell to his knees, face to the ground. Then he heard God's voice. Within the rainbow was Father God, in all His splendor. He was pure light, and there was nothing in the universe so grand, so glorious, and so wonderful. It was the climax of his experience, and he knew nothing would ever compare to it.

Jesus presented Rob by name, as He helped him up to his feet, before the Father. Rob wanted to fall on his face again before the Father, but Jesus held him upright.

Rob's reverence and sense of awe was intensified as the Father said "You are loved Rob, thank you for believing in My Son."

Rob took off his crown and cast it before Him and said; "I am forever in your debt for the grace you have shown me!"

Rob immediately knew and felt Him living within him, in the person of the Holy Spirit. He never quite understood what and how the Lord manifested His Spirit until that moment, when it was supernaturally revealed to him.

The Father then said, "I have been watching you before you were conceived. I know every cell in your body, and I'm well pleased with you Rob."

Jesus took Rob's crown and placed back on his head again, and said; "Welcome to your inheritance, you will reign with me forever. You are now co-heir to all the wonders of the Father. You will rule with Me along with those who call Me Lord and Savior. Your love will know no bounds, your deeds will give you everlasting joy, and your service will provide fulfillment beyond your understanding. We have much to do, and you will have forever to enjoy the riches that await you."

Rob was again speechless over the blissful surge he was experiencing.

Rob looked and saw the twenty-four thrones surrounding the Father. The seats were for the elders who represent the twelve tribes of Israel and the twelve apostles. Some of the seats were unoccupied and beckoned Rob to ask Jesus why?

Jesus knew what was going through his mind, and before he could ask, Jesus replied, "They are out in their mansions or enjoying fellowship with others."

Rob had remembered that in the book of Revelation, John had a vision where the elders represented were seated during the opening of the judgment scrolls.

Jesus then said; "It is not time for that prophecy to be fulfilled. That is yet to come."

Then the angelic host broke into a chorus that took Rob's breath away. How wonderful to stand before the Creator of the universe and to experience His pure love. As he took it in, he knew he was finally home and that this was only the beginning of an eternity of joy. He was experiencing relationship in its purest form. God, with him, in him, and for him, forever.

Two Ways to an End

As Rob looked around, he saw angels standing as far as he could see. The angels were so numerous that it was beyond counting them. The sight of a sea of these glorious beings in their various forms specific to their purpose was amazing. How awesome it is, he thought, to see and experience this moment. Rob saw other souls enter and fall before the Lord as he joined the chorus of angels. The collective joy of all who were coming and the thrill of being in the presence of God, made the encounter better than anything he had ever experienced.

Rob didn't know how long he had been there because time seemed to go so fast. He felt as if he could worship there forever.

An angel came and introduced himself to Rob. His name was Reveal, and he was Rob's guardian angel on earth.

As he led Rob out of God's throne room, Rob asked, "Where are we going?"

"We're going on a tour Rob," He replied.

"A tour of what?" Rob asked.

"The rest of heaven of course," he replied, as they walked away from God's throne.

"So you've been my guardian angel?" Rob asked.

"Yes," he replied, "I've been watching over you since you were in your mother's womb. I have always been by your side when you were in danger. I've protected you, kept you from evil, and helped you in your times of need. God sent me to aid you when you were in danger from the forces of darkness."

Rob was surprised and said, "I knew that angels watched over us, but I never realized that I had my own personal angel."

"Rob," he explained, "all of God's children have guardian angels that are sent to protect the elect. We were created to be ministering spirits, and our joy is to insure that God's children are not ravaged by the prince and principalities of the fallen world order. Satan seeks to destroy anyone who calls Jesus their Lord. He deceives the masses and without our intervention, would destroy every believer."

Reveal showed Rob the breath and scope of heaven and took him through gardens and buildings that were beyond description.

"Our Lord has been preparing this place for His children since Adam sinned in the garden," he said.

"His plan of restoration and redemption is perfect. This is what you were created for, to be by His side and rule the universe. I am so privileged to experience it with you."

Reveal didn't appear like the angels depicted in the paintings with giant wings and gentle faces. He was tall and strong and had a persona of power that Rob couldn't get over. He was a mighty warrior and was very humble. Rob liked him right away, because he was masculine and powerful, and Rob felt like a man around him. He had a glow that was different than Rob's own body, and a multi-dimensional appearance that reflected God's glory in a magnificent way.

He wasn't physical in the sense that he had a body that had substance; it was rather like, a transparent form that was filled with energy. As he moved, the appearance seemed to take on various forms, conforming to the environment and activity. He seemed to be able to manifest himself to his purpose in the moment. Like humans, he was unique and had an individual personality of his own.

Reveal introduced Rob to some of the other angels, and it was obvious that they had a special connection with one another. Their focus was always on serving God and His children. How thrilling it was to actually hang out with angels and understand their unique purpose.

Reveal then said, "Jesus asked that I spend this time with you, so that you will get to know me. Of course, I know you probably better than you know yourself Rob. As a ministering servant to God, I was created to meet your needs and guide you to your destination. It is my joy to finally communicate with you."

Rob wanted to know why humans couldn't see them when they were on earth.

Reveal replied, "That would create a dependency on us that negates the Lordship and dependence on God. Unfortunately for you, our abilities to be seen in the physical world are only allowed on a very limited basis from our Lord. There were a couple of times that unknowingly, I talked with you. I appeared as a man and gave you a message once."

"Remember when you were rear ended by that drunk driver?" he asked.

"I remember it like it was yesterday," Rob replied. "I thought I was going to die. Laura was in the passenger's seat, and I thought for sure she would be injured when I saw him in the rear view mirror, hitting us at full speed."

Reveal then said, "You and Laura would have been killed had I not slowed the truck down just before impact, and then cushioned you both in your seats."

"Really!" Rob exclaimed, "I always wondered how we escaped that wreck without a scratch, especially when they had to cut us out of the wreckage."

Rob asked him, "How many angels are there?" Reveal smiled, "More than there are humans, no one knows the number except God. I can tell you they are like the sands on the seashore, more than could ever be counted. The thing that amazes even me is that we are all different from one another. The variety and function of each of us was specifically designed by God for a unique purpose."

As Reveal concluded the tour, Rob asked if he could go back to God's throne. The wonders and beauty of heaven were so grand, Rob felt compelled to go back and proclaim His glory and worship Him. The riches and experiences were beyond anything Rob could have ever imagined on earth.

They were both suddenly there before the throne and Rob fell down and cried out, "Holy, Holy, Holy, the whole universe is filled with Your glory. Praises and honor and glory are Yours. Thank You for your grace, thank You for your love, thank You for Your plan. You are more wonderful than words can express."

Then a chorus of angels and saints sang songs of praise and thanksgiving unto the Lord.

Call to Art

The next morning in New York, Kate decided she should call Art to tell him the news about Rob's passing. She tried his office and Art's secretary indicated that he was at lunch. Kate had forgotten about the two hour time difference in New York. When Kate told her that Art's brother had passed away, she suggested that Kate might be able to reach Art on his cell phone.

Art was with his partner Adam, and they always used their lunchtime to review pending deals, and coordinate their assignments. Art made every minute count and never rested from his business deals. Adam was the same way, which is why he was a perfect partner for Art.

Adam was also divorced, and they would often play off each other as they dated women who would put up with their impersonal view on life, and their lack of commitment to a relationship. Never the less, they seemed to enjoy the chase, as they traded stories and sometimes relationships with women who liked the high visibility lifestyle that they enjoyed.

They both liked having parties at their penthouse apartments, where they could flaunt their success and make themselves the center of attention. Most women found them both charming and attractive, as they took the opportunity to exploit them. As their reputations became legendary, there were fewer and fewer women that would fall for their allure.

They would often drink themselves into a stupor, as they complained about the gold diggers that were part of the fast lane that consumed their world. Their lives were superficial and hollow. They thought that fulfilling their lustful pleasures would fill and satisfy them. Then toward the end, they would both succumb to the seedy world of nightclubs and private parties where no commitments were needed, only money. Their lifestyles were perverse and decadent.

It's amazing how deceitful money can become, as its power consumes and manipulates the souls of a men. The desires of the heart are deceitful beyond belief. The thoughts of men are wicked and evil. The desires of the flesh can't be satisfied. The lie that the world presents, leads to unhappiness and destruction.

Art rarely answered his calls while at lunch, but something prompted him to answer when Kate called.

When he answered, Kate began to weep, she said, "Art, I'm sorry to tell you that Rob passed away last night."

After a long period of silence, Art finally said, "I was going to come see him Kate, but I've just been too busy here at work to get away."

Kate knew that Art was just feeling guilty about Rob's passing, and said, "I understand Art. It would have been great if the two of you would have seen each other before Rob's passing."

"Art, I wanted to let you know that Rob wrote you a letter before he passed away. Rob wrote it, because he wanted to let you know how he felt about you, before he died."

"Art," she continued, "You know, he loved you so much.

He spent the last six weeks writing each day. The letter he wrote will tell you his heart."

It was all Kate could do to hold herself together. "You know Art, the past month Rob reminisced about how much fun you had as kids, and he so missed the closeness that you two experienced when you were young. I hope you read the letter when you get it, I mailed it yesterday, and you should have it either today or tomorrow." She said.

Art was now on the brink of tears, and replied, "I'll look for it tonight when I get home."

Art was on his second martini as part of his standard three-martini lunch. The reality of Rob's death hit him hard. He began to cry.

"I'm so sorry Kate, I miss the memories too. Rob was such a good man, so much better than me. It was hard for me to be around him, it made me feel bad about myself. I just want you to know, I only wish that I were half the man he was. Kate, the truth is I have always been envious of his life. If I could do it over again, I would do it differently."

"Kate," he asked, "Is there anything that I can do for you?"

Kate told him, "Between me and the kids, we seem to have things under control. Rob had everything mapped out for us knowing that he would be gone soon." She replied.

Kate asked, "Will you come out for the memorial service? It will be this Saturday at our church."

"Kate, of course I'll come; I promise I'll be there." He replied.

Then Kate also asked him, "Will you be willing to say a few words about Rob?"

"I'd be honored. Kate, I'll fly out Friday and review with you what I will be sharing."

Kate was elated and said, "Thank you Art for your support and for coming. I know it would have meant so much to Rob. Please call me when you have a chance to read his letter."

Art said, "I promise I'll call you as soon as I receive and read it."

"I'm calling everyone I can think of, Art, if you can think of anyone else that should know about Rob's passing, could you contact them?"

"I'll go through my address book and call some old classmates and childhood friends that would want to know." Art replied.

Then Kate said, "Thank you Art, I'll talk with you tomorrow."

As Art finished the phone call, he looked up, and realized that he had forgotten about his partner being there while he took the call. Art's partner, Adam was shocked about Art's brother.

"I didn't know your brother was ill," he said.

Art seemed to tense up as he said, "He had terminal cancer."

Adam said, "It's strange that you never mentioned it to me."

Art looked frustrated, and then said, "I preferred not to think about it. It hits to close to home, because I am his older brother and age is creeping up on me. When I heard about Rob's cancer, I decided the best thing for me would be to stay away. Who wants to be depressed by being around someone who is dying?"

"Wow Art, that's a pretty cold response, even for you."Adam replied.

Art ordered another martini and after a few seconds said, "Hey Adam, would you mind if I spent some time alone? I just need to think about some things for a bit."

Adam said, "Sure, I know you've got a lot on your mind. I need to get back to the office anyway because those closing documents need to be signed and returned to the attorneys today.

You should go home and forget about your work. Art, I know you, and you need to process this. Based on all the stories you told me about you two as kids, you will need to grieve. I can take care of the deals, and I can reach you by phone if I need you."

Art sat and thought for a minute, and said, "You know you're probably right, I think I'll go to the gym and take a nice steam as I decompress. Thanks for your understanding. I know you will take care of business until I am back to normal."

Adam looked at Art, and said, "Hey buddy, if you have any more to drink, call a cab."

Art replied, "Yah, yah, I know, I'll take your advice if I get woozy."

Adam asked the waiter to give Rob some space, and then he left for the office.

Art ordered a fourth martini and started thinking about Rob and his regrets about shutting Rob out of his life. He was ashamed that he had not gone to see Rob before he died or even bothered to call him. As the alcohol took effect, he started to lose control of his emotions.

The waiter asked if he was okay, and Art realized that people were starting to notice his obvious grief.

Art frequented the restaurant most days, and he knew most everyone there. Showing his emotions was not something the staff had ever experienced from him. Art collected himself after downing the balance of the fourth martini, and asked for the check.

As he staggered out to his new Ferrari in the parking garage, he began to think about their childhood memories. An hour passed as he sat in his car to collect himself. He remembered all the great times he enjoyed with Rob.

Thoughts of all their crazy adventures and the fun they shared growing up, filled his mind.

Art cried out in anger and yelled "Why?" As the thoughts welled up in him he began to weep with grief.

Art had buried his memories deep inside. He thought about all of the games and challenges he and his brother experienced during their childhood. His grief over the loss of his brother, made him angry. He thought that God had robbed him of the relationship he once had with Rob.

The last time he had really thought about those memories was while he was dating his first wife. It was just after graduating college. His soon-to-be wife, wanted to know why he and his brother didn't talk with each other. The way Art told the story from his standpoint, prompted her to encourage him to sit down with Rob and tell him how he felt. Looking back upon it now, he should have given Rob an opportunity to hear him out. From Art's viewpoint, his brother had abandoned him in college, when he stopped hanging out with him.

He told her about how they did everything together as boys. Art felt abandoned, when Rob stopped going out drinking with him in college. Rob didn't seem to be the same guy that he once knew. His outlook was so different after he started going to that Bible study. Rob's new conversion to Christianity drove a wedge between their lifestyles. Art blamed Rob's Christianity, for their separation. The entire situation made Art bitter and angry, blaming Rob completely for their separation. Art disliked everything Rob believed and was represented in his lifestyle.

After Rob met Kate, it seemed to Art, that his brother didn't care about him anymore because he was consumed with her and his religion, so they stopped communicating. The resentment intensified when Rob tried to push his beliefs on Art. Art would have nothing to do with what he called, "the brainwashing of Jesus freaks."

As Art pulled out of the parking garage, more thoughts of the good times that filled their childhood emerged, making him morn again over his loss. His emotions were running wild and he started sobbing uncontrollably. As he turned onto the freeway tunnel, he ran a red light, and a semi truck hit him square in the driver's side.

The truck was only going about forty miles per hour, but the small Ferrari was no match for the fully loaded truck. Art was instantly knocked unconscious at impact As soon as the police arrived; they immediately called to get special equipment that would allow them to cut Art out of his car. The policemen who arrived first on the scene instantly thought that based upon the amount blood everywhere, and by the condition of the car, it would be a miracle if anyone was alive in the wreckage.

Art's car was sandwiched under the front of the trucks cab, leaving no room to reach him. The fire department arrived with a large winch to pry the truck off the car. It was almost a half hour before they were able to pull the truck off the flattened Ferrari. As they removed the truck, the vast amount of blood splattered on the driver's crushed body made it difficult to see his condition. It was obvious that if the driver was alive, there would be serious injuries.

The driver's door was pushed in toward the center and the hood of the car totally sheered off. The glass was shattered and scattered everywhere. The driver of the truck was unharmed in the accident. As the car was revealed, he shook his head and said, "I can't believe he blew that stop light like that. I tried to stop but with the heavy load, it was futile. He must have been on a suicide mission the way he was flying through the intersection."

As they were working on the wreckage, the police officers took notes from the eye witnesses on the scene. They confirmed the driver's story that the driver of the Ferrari had run the stop light at an accelerated speed. After measuring the skid marks from the truck, they scurried to reroute the traffic and make room for the heavy equipment that would remove the wreckage and free the driver.

Pulling the Plug

As they reached into check for a pulse, they could see that although he had a weak pulse, he was losing blood rapidly. Art's body was riddled with lacerations and protruding bones. After an hour of cutting and prying the car apart, they were able to pull Art out onto a stretcher. Art was unconscious and had been badly crushed. His head and face were swollen and bruised. The paramedics stabilized him as they rushed him to the hospital.

In the ER, they assessed the damage and immediately put him on life support. Art had lost a dangerous amount of blood, so the doctors gave him three units of blood as they tried to stop the bleeding. There was no brain activity and without life support, the doctors would not be able to stop the bleeding to stabilize his condition.

The injuries to his shattered bones would require surgery, but with the condition of his head injuries and having no brain function, the decision to go further would need to fall on the immediate family. After administering life support and blood, they moved him to intensive care. Art had a business card in his wallet, but nothing that would tell them who to call in the event of an emergency. The admissions clerk called his office to get the number of his immediate family to let them know of his critical condition.

When Art's secretary asked why they needed that information, the clerk was vague. The clerk explained that Art had been involved in an automobile accident, and indicated that he was at Mount Sinai Hospital. Art's secretary transferred her to his partner, because she didn't have any of Art's family information.

When Art's partner, Adam answered, he couldn't believe it, "I was just with him a couple of hours ago at lunch!" he exclaimed.

The admissions clerk indicated that it was vital that they reach his family. Adam remembered that Art had names of every client and other contact information in his computer database. He figured that he might also have his daughter's number or his ex-wives in the database as well.

He was surprised to see that none of his ex-wives were in Art's database. The only family member he could find was his daughter Courtney. Adam didn't know very much about Art's family or personal life, because Art never talked about them. It was all business whenever they were together, and Art was very private about his daughter and his previous marriages.

Art worked from the time he woke up, until he went to sleep each night. He had dinner engagements most nights with business associates leaving very little time for family involvement. After giving the number that he did have to the hospital, he decided he should also have Art's secretary try to find every family member she could, by looking through Art's office. He did know that his only child was now an adult, in law school, and that the other marriages were cloaked in hostility and hatred toward one another. The phone number of his 26-year-old daughter was in the computer and it was his best bet to reach the rest of his family.

Adam was about to call the hospital to provide them with the phone number of Art's daughter Courtney. But decided to call Courtney first himself. She was in her final year of law school at Columbia University. As she answered the phone, he realized that he would be the first to give her the bad news, and he was sorry that he had made the call.

"Courtney?" he asked.

"Yes," she replied, not recognizing his voice,

"This is Adam Feldman, your father's business partner. The reason for my call is that I wanted you to know that the hospital needs to get in touch with you. I'm afraid your father has been in a serious automobile accident, and the hospital is trying to find members of his immediate family to discuss his situation. The hospital will not give me any specifics because I am not a member of his family."

Courtney was silent for a few seconds and then said, "I haven't talked with my father in three years and it was not a pleasant conversation when I did."

Adam explained that because she is his only child, and because he's divorced, she would be the next of kin.

Courtney thought for a moment and then said, "I'm only a couple of miles from the hospital, so I'll just go there to see what they need." She thanked him and said that she would contact her mother, as soon as she knew what was going on.

On the way to the hospital, she called her mom to let her know that she was on her way to the hospital. Her mom answered but seemed perturbed that Courtney was involved. Her marriage ended badly when she took a substantial portion of Art's assets in the divorce. She hadn't spoken to him in twelve years. She didn't think it was right to put this burden on her daughter and decided that she would contact the other ex-wives to meet her and Courtney at the hospital.

When Courtney got to the hospital they were relieved that she was there. They confirmed that she was legally the next of kin. The doctors explained Art's condition, and advised her that the sight might be traumatic. The hospital wanted someone to make the decision about Art's life support and care. Courtney barely knew her dad and wasn't sure what to do under the circumstance. Knowing the law, Courtney acknowledged that it was her legal responsibility to decide whether to continue life support. She decided to call her mom and ask her to meet her there at the hospital before she went in to see her dad. Her mom told her that she had contacted Art's other ex-wives and persuade them to meet her at the hospital. Fortunately, they all lived in New York and were able to come right away under the circumstance. Art's other marriages ended similar to his first, but prenuptial agreements simplified the divorces. None of them had warm feelings toward Art.

Once they all arrived at the hospital, all of them went into Art's room to see his condition and to consult with the doctors. Art was now very pale and the swelling from the impact made it hard to recognize him. When they looked at him, they gasped and couldn't believe it was really Art. The decision came easy when his last wife said that he had told her several years ago that if he were ever injured so badly that he wouldn't be able to function in a normal fashion, he wouldn't want to live.

Courtney could tell from the doctors that Art would not get better, and it really was a matter of time before he would die regardless of the treatment.

She asked the doctor, "If it were you, would you take him off life support?"

He said that he would rather not answer that question, but she could tell by the way he said it, that it would be affirmative.

Courtney asked how long he would live without life support. The doctor told her his best guess would be at most, only a couple of hours. She asked if they would all stay with her until Art passed away. They all agreed to stay with her. She then told the doctors to take him off life support.

Art's partner arrived and was shocked to learn of Art's hopeless condition. When he saw him he was stunned by the sight and panicked as he thought about how vital Art was to their business. He excused himself and left the hospital overwhelmed. He surprised himself as he became emotional and realized that he had feelings for Art. The loss would make a huge difference in the deals that were pending, and his loss would change the course of their business. More than that, he had grown close to Art and genuinely loved working with him. They were more than partners they were friends. Their lives were consumed and revolved around their business.

Within an hour of removing the life support, they pronounced Art dead. It was more of a relief when the ordeal was over, and they could go home to their families. Courtney roomed with a girlfriend but was so busy with school that she avoided any meaningful relationships with men. Her mom had remarried and had two other children with her second husband. The other two ex-wives also remarried and the youngest was six months pregnant.

The gravity of Courtney's responsibility in having to make arrangements for her father's burial overwhelmed her. The thought of involving herself in her father's affairs gripped her as she drove back to her apartment. She didn't know who to contact or what s he should do about any of it, so she decided to call her law professor who she had interned with that summer. After receiving some advice about getting legal counsel and telling her to remain strong Courtney thanked him and hung up the phone, still unsure about what she would do next.

The events of the day exhausted her, and the gruesome appearance of her Dad replayed in her mind. She knew that the sight of him lying there would haunt her the rest of her life. The thoughts of choosing law rather than a medical degree were confirmed as she thought about the horrific scenes that doctors see on a daily basis.

That evening, Courtney told her roommate Rebecca what had transpired. Rebecca seemed shocked at how well Courtney was handling the trauma. She asked her if it would be alright if she prayed with her for comfort. Courtney welcomed the idea of allowing God to help her through her grief.

"Thank you," she replied, "I'm so glad that you're here with me."

Rebecca asked the Lord to help Courtney through her grief and to allow her to see God's supernatural intervention in her life.

Courtney skipped her classes and spent the day making phone calls and visiting her father's business partner. Since she would be taking care of his estate and funeral arrangements, she thought it was important to learn what she could about her Dad's business and personal affairs. Art's partner gave Courtney the address where her father lived. Courtney decided that going to her dad's apartment might reveal some answers about his estate.

His home was on the upper east side of Fifth Avenue. It was strange that after all these years, she had never visited him at his home. Their strained relationship made going to his home very stressful. She knew it was just a matter of time before she would need to go there to settle his affairs. Going there now would make the anticipation brief. She was exhausted and emotionally drained but decided to deal with it now.

So many thoughts raced through her mind as she realized that in spite of their strained relationship, she was really the only family member that still cared for her Dad. Some of her memories of him when she was young made her weep as she drove home. It was all she could do to make it to her bed. As she opened the door to an empty apartment, she broke down and fell face down into her bed. How she wished her roommate was there with her, but she was visiting her mom on Long Island and would be gone for the night.

Art's home was only about a twenty-minute drive from her apartment and she knew hoped to find her Dad's will, or any other helpful paperwork he might have kept there. She also found out from her visit to his office, that Art used the same attorney for all three divorces, and he might know if Art had any trusts or wills. When she pulled up to the building, a doorman opened her door and asked who she was there to see. She explained the situation, and the doorman told her that he would need to get authorization to open his flat to her. The doorman called the manager of the building, and he came down to discuss her access to Art's apartment. Courtney had presented a death certificate, and a statement regarding her relationship with her Dad.

It was a shock to both the building manager and the doorman when they heard the news. Art was rarely home and wasn't very friendly to the people who were there. The manager and doorman seemed pleased that Art would not be coming home. When the manager opened the flat and gave her the key, he told her that he would let the staff know that she would be visiting and until she figured out what to do, she could come and go as she liked. As she entered the flat, it gave her an eerie feeling and a chill went through her body. The flat was appointed with ultra modern furniture and everything was perfectly in its' place. It was almost as if nobody lived there. It was a large flat with four bedrooms, a study and large living areas.

Given his lifestyle, it seemed strange that he had such a large place. As she looked around, she noticed a laptop computer and opened it. Some of Art's computer programs were opened revealing several spreadsheets of various portfolios. The computer also revealed recent emails to and from his attorney. Courtney looked through the file cabinet in his study and found a host of legal documents, stock certificates, and property deeds. The call to his attorney revealed that Art had most everything in writing, and that Courtney was the only heir in his will. His attorney handled most of his holdings. He was more than accommodating to continue the relationship with Courtney, knowing she would receive the majority of his assets.

When Courtney was leaving, the doorman handed her the mail from the past three days. Most of the mail consisted of statements from his stock portfolios and holdings. Then she noticed a hand written envelope from her Dad's brother Rob. She was not aware that her Dad's brother had died. She decided that she would read the letter later because she needed to touch base with her mom and the other family members about what she learned.

Later, as Courtney opened the letter, she was interrupted by a call from her Dad's partner.

"Hello Courtney is this a good time?" He asked.

"Yes I was just sitting down to read a letter that my dad received from his brother."

Adam was surprised that there was a letter from Art's brother Rob, because he knew that he was dead.

"Courtney, that's what I was calling about. Just before your Dad's accident, he received a call from Rob's wife letting him know that his brother had died."

Courtney had never met Rob, but she remembered some of the stories that her dad had told her as a young girl about their childhood adventures. Courtney thanked him for the information and for his thoughtfulness.

The letter was several hand written pages long. As she unfolded the paper, a small gold cross fell from the envelope. As she began to read the letter, she could tell that the letter was written with compassion and love. The words gripped her as she continued to read. Rob was reaching out to his brother in love and sought to mend their strained relationship. She couldn't help thinking how loving her uncle was toward her father, who was so difficult. Making the effort to open his heart, touched her as she read.

Courtney had been invited to a church by her roommate and although she was intrigued to know more, she decided that she was too busy to take the two hours away from her law studies. Rebecca read the Bible all the time and seemed to be so happy in spite of the many tragedies that seemed to follow her through her young life.

Reading the letter became more difficult as she continued along. Learning how wonderful their relationship was as boys made her think that she should have made an effort to know her Dad. Courtney realized that her bitterness toward her Dad was rooted in the pain of her mom's separation and divorce that ended poorly. Courtney teared up with emotion when Rob explained why he was reaching out to Art for the last time and that he wouldn't be able to reach out very much longer. As she finished the letter, she broke down and fell to her knees.

"Lord," she prayed, "I don't know much about you, but I want to know more. Help me to love like Rob loved. I know I've been selfish and have ignored you. Help me to understand."

As she was praying, Rebecca came in. Rebecca could hardly believe her eyes as she quietly knelt beside her. Courtney was crying as she clasped the letter.

Rebecca asked if she was okay, and Courtney replied,

"I'm not sure what I'm experiencing, but it seemed to free me from my grief."

As Rebecca read the letter, she realized that Courtney had experienced God's intervention in her life and that she received God's gift of salvation.

Her joy was contagious as they hugged and held each other closely.

Rebecca said, "I've been praying for you Courtney, I know that your Dads' passing was very hard on you, and I've been praying that you would have strength through this trial."

Courtney replied, "I have so many questions about what I've just experienced. I would like you to take me to your church this Sunday, if it's alright with you?"

"Absolutely," she replied, "It would be my joy to help you draw close to God."

Rebecca gave Courtney a Bible and began to explain what was happening to her and how it would change her life. Rebecca seemed to have such a clear way of explaining Spiritual things to her. As she read the passages in the Bible, she asked Jesus into her heart. The two of them were joyfully crying, as a peace fell upon her that she had never experienced before. She knew that everything would be okay and that her father's death brought her to a place where she needed God. Everything was good and as she dosed off into a deep sleep, Rebecca prayed that Courtney would be used in a mighty way.

The next morning, Courtney decided to call her Aunt Kate. Rob had written her cell phone number at the bottom of the letter. And Courtney knew that she would not be aware of Art's death.

Kate answered the phone right away thinking it might be Art calling to let her know that he was in town.

"Hi Aunt Kate, this is Courtney, Art's daughter. I'm calling because I need to let you know that my Dad died yesterday in a car accident."

Kate was stunned by the call and was unable to speak at first. Courtney began to cry when she explained that Art never read Rob's letter, and that she had read the letter.

"Kate," she said, "Uncle Rob's letter was so loving and moving that I prayed to receive Jesus into my life, and make him my Lord. I'm so sorry that my Dad didn't read Rob's letter, because I know how much my dad loved him. I remember the stories my dad told me about them when I was a little girl. He would talk about Rob all the time.

Kate collected herself and asked if she was okay.

Courtney started to break down with emotion as she said, "If it wasn't for Rob's letter, I'm not sure I could have emotionally handled what happened. I am so grateful that God allowed me to read it. I'm not sure why God's timing was what it was, but I'm trusting that there's a greater purpose. I know you're busy with Rob's passing, and I will be making arrangements for my dad's memorial service."

They both started to sob uncontrollably.

Kate finally said, "God's ways are not our ways. Courtney, I know this must all be overwhelming for you, but you will come to trust His ways as you develop your relationship with Him. Please let me know if there is anything I can do to help."

Courtney said, "Thank you for sharing your heart with me. I would love to continue our conversation later if it's okay with you. I'll call you after things settled down."

Kate said, "You're welcome to call me whenever you would like. I would also like to invite you to come visit me. I know both Rob and your dad would want us to get to know each other."

"Thank you Kate, I'll call you in a few days." She replied.

The following morning, Rebecca asked Courtney to go

to a Bible study that she and three other girls held at the Starbucks next to their building. She was thrilled that she had Rebecca and her friends there to share her new faith. The study turned out to be just what Courtney needed knowing that she had so much to do and that the burden of her dad's burial and memorial service would fall on her. She was also apprehensive about what being an heir to her dad's businesses would mean, and how it would change her life. She wondered how her new faith in God would alter her plans. Trusting God was difficult and foreign to Courtney, and it made her nervous at first.

After her time with her new friends she scheduled an appointment with her father's attorney, Mr. Spellman.

The offices of her dad's attorney, was elaborate and ornate. The rich woods and dark hues set the tone of wealth and power. As she sat in the lobby waiting for the owner of the large firm to greet her, she could see several attorneys in the conference room with several stacks of papers spread across the table.

Mr. Spellman came out to greet her and Courtney said, "Thank you for meeting with me so soon."

Mr. Spellman replied, "It's our pleasure, and we hope that we can continue the great relationship we enjoyed with your father. Come into the conference room, we have everything prepared In anticipation of your arrival.

As she entered the conference room, she counted nine attorneys each with their own portfolio of papers. At the end of the table was Mr. Spellman's partner Saul Goldstein who specialized in the tax and estate law.

Mr. Spellman began by introducing each attorney and what specialty they handled for her dad's holdings.

Mr. Spellman began, "Because your father's holding were so diverse and sizable, our firm divided the assets into various entities and trusts. This will minimize the estate taxes while allowing you to control these assets. It's a bit complicated, and we will need the power of attorney to transact some of the filings for you. Your father put complete trust in our firm to transact his dealings. He was our largest client, and a valued friend. The total holdings of his assets in round numbers are just over a billion dollars. Courtney was shocked at the size of her dad's estate. The amount actually scared her as she tried not to seem too surprised. The documents that exercised her control of the estate were signed and notarized. The meeting lasted more than three hours, absent of some specific details, so Courtney could grasp the overall picture of her dad's estate.

As Courtney left the room, she felt overwhelmed and frightened at the scope of her new responsibilities. She would need to meet with Art's partner to discuss her role in their partnership and how that would impact her.

Courtney thanked them all and told them that she would meet with each of them within a couple of weeks, after the affairs of her dad's passing were completed.

The ride back to her apartment seemed to take forever. As she entered the apartment Rebecca was just getting back from her class. Rebecca was also finishing up her graduate degree and would be entering the business world with an MBA. As she came in, Rebecca could tell that Courtney was overwhelmed.

"You look like you could use a hug," she said.

Rebecca pulled Courtney in and gave her a long, firm hug. Courtney was thankful that she was there for comfort and encouragement.

Rebecca welcomed the conversation as Courtney reviewed the events of the day. Courtney asked if she would help her sort out the details of her father's burial and memorial service. The impact of all her new responsibilities seemed overwhelming, and Rebecca was more than happy to support her in any way she could. Their relationship was instantly bonded by her new faith in God.

Courtney felt closer to Rebecca now than she had to anyone in a long time.

Courtney looked at Rebecca and said, "Thank you so much for being such a great friend. I don't think I would have made it through all this without you."

Rebecca replied, "It's my pleasure to be used by God, and I know He put us together for a greater purpose."

Time flew by as they planned and coordinated the final details for her father's memorial service. Eventually, they both fell into a deep sleep exhausted from the day.

Rob's Memorial Service

It was early Saturday morning, and Kate didn't sleep well, as she anticipated the day ahead of her. Not having Rob next to her in bed became harder as each night passed. The reality of how much she would miss him was overwhelming. As she stirred during the night, she reached for Rob, but he wasn't there. Kate clasped Rob's pillow and could smell his scent as she clutched it tightly. She couldn't help thinking about the call she had received the day before about Art's death. Rob would have felt so sad knowing that Art was dead. Then she prayed that she would be able to make it through the day ahead of her. Soon, she began to feel the Lord comfort her.

It was a rainy spring morning and the drizzle seemed appropriate for the occasion. Kate didn't understand why the Lord would take Art in such a violent way and why now. The thought of him not reading Rob's letter made it even more depressing. Kate knew that Art was probably in hell. As she opened her Bible and read Psalm 139, she was comforted knowing that Rob was in a much better place and was no longer in pain. The inspirational words were exactly what she needed to strengthen her for the memorial service ahead.

Kate's daughter made most of the funeral and memorial service arrangements and prepared the photos that would be shown spanning Rob's life, prepared in a video montage. Kate hadn't seen it yet and felt that it would be a perfect way for her to remember Rob. She was glad that they had spent so much of their time over the past couple of months scanning and categorizing the photos. Remembering all the great times they experienced together softened her grief as she began the day.

They decided to have a small funeral for Rob on the following Monday with just the immediate family. In place of an open casket, a photo of Rob would be projected on a screen. Having Rob on display in a funeral home or at the church was not the way Rob wanted to be remembered. The cancer had taken a toll on his body and as he dwindled away, his face became drawn and hollow. The picture of Rob on the screen when he was healthy was a better memory of him.

Kate showered and made herself ready for the day. Her daughter picked her up at 9:30 a.m., allowing plenty of time to greet people before the 11:00 a.m. memorial service. As people streamed in, it was all Kate could do to keep her emotions together. The number of people who came for Rob's service made Kate realize how loved Rob was and how many lives he had touched. She wondered if he was able see them from heaven as the people filed into the Chapel. Then she realized that any love that they could show him would be paled compared to that of the Lord. She had peace knowing Rob was truly in a better place.

As Kate walked down the aisle, she was taken back because the worship center was almost full. Several hundred people came to comfort the family and pay their respects. Many of Rob's clients were also there, and she knew that for many of them, this would be an opportunity to hear about Rob's spiritual journey for the first time.

She prayed that some of them would hear the gospel and make a profession of faith, as a result of what they were about to hear. Her daughter nudged her as some of Rob's old classmates entered the worship center and made their way to their seats.

The service started with a reading from Revelation 23 about heaven. Ryan, the worship pastor, sang a beautiful song that was comforting. Next, Kate's daughter shared how her Dad was so loving to her, and to his two grandchildren. Even to the end of his life while in all that pain, he was a model of joy and love for them to remember him. Laura read from Psalm 23 and ended by asking her to children to come and say goodbye to their Papa.

As they came up to the microphone, they were smiling. Rob's granddaughter, Jen spoke first. She read a poem that she had written to her Papa.

"Papa my best friend
To heaven God sends
A place that has no end
And love with God we send
Papa, the greatest to the end
We'll see you soon again
Love your little Jen"

Then David, his 8-year-old grandson came and said he would keep his picture on his bedroom wall so he could dream about having fun with him again soon. He didn't seem to actually realize that his Papa wouldn't be coming back. He had drawn a picture of them going down the hill and said that he would draw him another one, and mail it to him in heaven.

"I love you Papa! Everyone clapped as they exited the podium.

Rob's employer Stan was next. He couldn't keep his emotions in as he reached the podium.

"For those of you who don't know me, I had the privilege of having Rob as my sales manager, and more importantly, as my best friend. The impact that Rob has had on my life is insurmountable. Rob's presence made my business fun and exciting. His contagious joy reached everyone he met. I see many of our clients have come here because they too loved Rob. It is said that the character of a man is measured by the things he does that won't bring him gain, recognition, or personal pleasure. Rob's life was mostly about living that out. He always put others before himself. I loved him, his employees loved him, our clients loved him, and even the people that first met him, immediately loved him. There is no one that I know of that was an enemy of Rob. I know for many of you, his death leaves a gap that can't be replaced. I grieve because he will be missed by me and all of us here. I rejoice because I know God has a special place for Rob, and he is now in paradise."

"I come before you today knowing that I can only hope to live out the rest of my life as Rob lived his. He showed me that the truest happiness comes from relationships first with God, and then, with others."

"I am confident that Rob is now standing before his maker who is rewarding him saying; well done good and faithful servant."

As Stan left the podium, a video began to play with photos from Rob when he was an infant, then as a toddler. He was a chubby baby with a smile that seemed to be affixed to his face. Then came photos of him in his early years. The photos were of him and his brother together. It was as if they were never apart, and the look on each of their faces spoke volumes about their relationship. You could see the mischievous adventuresome spirit in each photo. As Rob entered his early teen years, you could see that Art was becoming less and less a part of Rob's life. Their age separation seemed to create a divide that they would never get back.

Rob was a short pudgy teen and looked much younger than his age. He worked hard to get good grades and had lots of close friends. Art was tall and slender and seemed to always be with a new girlfriend in the photos as they were displayed. In Rob's junior year of high school, he grew six inches, and his pudgy look disappeared. Rob ran for class president in his senior year and won. The photos showed that Rob was following in his brother's footsteps, who was very handsome and popular.

As they grew into adulthood, they were pictured together similar to their early years. The photos of their early college years revealed their crazy lifestyle of partying and debauchery. While these photos seemed somewhat shocking and out of Rob's character, they would be explained through the reading of Rob's letter to his brother by Kate, later in the service. There were photos showing them both drunk and hanging onto several girls, with beer bottles raised high and wearing toga costumes. Then the photos of Rob were absent of Art. It was as if Art was gone from Rob's life.

The photos of Rob's later college years were most often in groups and always included his new Christian friends. The photos revealed a new more serious look that projected an inner joy that contrasted to his prior photos of a hedonistic lifestyle.

Then the photos revealed him with Kate at a camp retreat. Every photo from there on during their remaining college years, she was by his side. They looked so happy, and you could tell that their love was much more than their initial physical attraction. Photos of their wedding and Rob dancing with various family members and friends brought laughter from the crowd.

Photos of them fixing up their little house in Wheaton made his humble manner unmistakable. The photos of him and his daughter Laura showed the love that he had for her and how he was continuously trying to make her into a little boy. As she grew older, the magic remained in their relationship. Their vacations revealed how they felt, as their expressions of love were obvious in every photo. Then as Laura entered her teen years, the photos reverted back to just Kate and him, as Laura started exerting her independence. Years seemed to slip by because there were fewer occasions for taking photos. The pictures of family holidays and gatherings revealed that Art was no longer around.

Then, photos of Laura's wedding with Rob walking her down the isle and looking into his daughter's eyes, with a smile of approval and joy filled the screen. Then photos of him and their grandchildren showed the return of his boyish personality. The photos showed him having fun and making the kids feel special. They seemed to have a uninhibited quality that you would expect in an advertisement. As the grandkids grew older, Rob's features seemed to change abruptly as his body progressed ahead of his youthful mentality.

Rob's receding hairline seemed to change rapidly. His thinning hair dramatically changed Rob's appearance. As his hair thinned he cut it shorter and shorter until he had a crew cut. The kids liked feeling his short hair and laughed whenever they felt it. The photos of the three of them together showed the special bond that only a grandfather could have with his grandchildren. Intermixed were photos of his co-workers and friends at various functions and celebrations. You could see that he was adored by all, and his happy-go-lucky persona was contagious. Many of the photos were of Stan and him, as their friendship grew and they seemed to be together all the time.

Two Ways to an End

Some of the photos of Rob's classes and Bible studies showed that he truly cared for everyone. He never favored one person over another, but treated everyone equally with respect and love. The Church would miss his teaching but even more than that, they would miss the way he cared for them. As the final photos appeared, It was him hugging various people who came to see him in his final days. The music, which was upbeat and energetic, slowed to a soft reflective tune that faded away as the photos ended.

Kate approached the podium being helped by her son in-law. The emotions of the photomontage were more than she could process. The memories of their life seemed to pass before her very eyes making her realize the brevity of life. She knew that the letter she was about to read would impact many lives, and that its' essence would be expressed in his own words. The love that was from God spoke volumes about Rob's character. As she walked up, she asked the Lord to strengthen her. A supernatural calm came over her as she began to speak.

"I'm about to read you a letter that Rob wrote to his brother Art. The letter never made it to Art, because he died in a car accident the day after Rob passed away. God works in mysterious ways, and I know that he would want the letter read for those who may end up like Art, separated from God forever. I have prayed that the letter would be used for a much greater good, and I stand before you, and my God, knowing that Rob's life is manifested in this letter."

Kate read the letter, and as she read it you could see many weep and reflect upon, their own individual life. There were smiles of joy and tears of sorrow as she read with conviction and expression. Rob's words were reflective and comforting. The sound of weeping filled the sanctuary and many were praying as she read. Each word seemed as if it were directly from God. As she finished the letter, the

Pastor came and invited people to pray to receive Jesus into their heart. Over 30 people came to faith in Jesus Christ that day, as music was played.

The music with everyone singing together made the place feel like heaven itself. Tears fell from just about everyone there, and the music played for several minutes before it drew to an end.

As people walked out, they knew that the presence of God fell upon them and that place. The entire experience was beyond description or words. The power of God can't contain experiences like the one revealed that day. People would tell others of their experience that day, and especially those that had given their lives to Jesus.

Kate invited everyone to her home for a catered luncheon after the service. Many people came and filled the house. She realized how blessed to be his wife and the years she had with such a special man. Joy blessed her to see that his life had an eternal impact and was filled with memories that she would cherish for the rest of her days. The thought of knowing that she would be with him again one day, made it a joyful time.

Banquet

Jesus came as Rob was worshipping at the throne. Rob seemed surprised when Jesus interrupted him. He said, "Come with me Rob, I have a surprise for you."

Jesus took Rob to a large golden archway that lead into a fabulous garden. There were hundreds of angels at various stations within the garden. They were all stunning in appearance and majesty. Rob was taken back by the fact that they were all much larger than people in stature and power. Varying in height from eight to ten feet, they were magnificent. Their bodies glowed with radiance and vitality. Each seemed to have a unique quality that emanated from them as they ministered to the needs of the people. They were preparing and serving food to everyone who were seated at golden tables dispersed throughout the garden.

Rob instantly thought that it was odd that angels, who appeared more magnificent than people were serving them.

Jesus knew Rob was wondering about the angels and their majesty. He looked at Rob and said, "We created the angels to be ministering spirits to us. They love serving us; it is their passion. Each of them knows their special purpose and plan within the Father's will. They have learned from the fall of Satan and his followers, that anything outside of the Father's will only leads to unhappiness and discontentment. The fall and rebellion of Satan's followers serves as a warning to the faithful to live for the very purpose for which He created them. Because I became a man and have redeemed mankind, their desire is to also serve mankind who are now co-heirs with Me."

Rob saw that there were about 100 people dispersed throughout the banquet. Everyone seemed to be enjoying their intimate fellowship with one another. Their fellowship seemed to go deeper, leaving Rob with the desire to experience the same type of relationship.

Conversations conducted from mind to mind, made their thoughts more personal as they communicated with one another. He was amazed that although they were speaking without sound, the personality unique to each person was retained and recognized by the hearer. It was an enhanced form of themselves that was unmistakably communicated in their purest form. As they exchanged thoughts with one another, multiple conversations could occur simultaneously. The expansive capacity of their unobstructed thoughts could multitask mentally, while they enjoyed listening to beautiful music while they were communicating.

As Rob entered the center of the garden, two angels sounded trumpets and announced Rob's arrival. Everyone rose to their feet and clapped as Rob entered in astonishment.

At first, Rob wasn't sure who all these people were who clapped with joy as he was welcomed.

 Jesus said, "Rob, I have prepared a banquet in your honor. Welcome to your first banquet!" Rob's Mom and Dad were seated at the center of the room and between then was a large golden throne adorned in jewels.

"Come son and sit with us," his Dad said.

Rob seemed embarrassed by the fuss they were making

over him and the honor that was bestowed upon him.

Jesus knew that Rob would try to dismiss the accolades and said, "Rob, you affected many lives on earth, and you were, are, and will be in the future, instrumental in the Father's plans. You may not recognize many of these people, because they look so different here. Everyone here at the banquet has been impacted either directly, or indirectly, as a result of the righteous deeds you did on earth. As more people pass from their present state, into their eternal state, they will join us at these banquets, making your sphere of influence larger."

As Rob looked more closely at some of the people sitting at the perimeter tables, he began to recognize and recall why they were there.

At the table next to his was a man that he remembered helping on Sundays when communion was served. He would help him take communion because he was unable to take the elements himself. He was afflicted and unable to lift the juice to his lips without spilling it all over himself. He was suffered with MS, and Rob observed his frustration as he tried to lift the elements. Rob noticed his struggle and had offered to serve him the cup by pouring it into his mouth. As Rob recognized him, the man rose to his feet and walked over to thank him for serving him.

Rob couldn't get over how different he looked now and how dramatic the transformation was, now that he was rid of his physical body. As he stood, Rob was surprised by how tall he was. He had only seen him in his wheelchair and never realized that he was a very tall man.

He smiled and said, "you may not have known this when you were serving me communion, but that small act of kindness is what kept me coming back to Church. At first I was angry that God would allow me to suffer the way He did. It was your servanthood that made me yield to Him and accept the trial and ask for forgiveness. I owe you so much, Rob. I am sitting here in paradise with a perfect body that I will enjoy forever because of your love and compassion."

Rob blushed and said, "It was my pleasure to serve you, because it made me realize how blessed I was that God had given me good health. Your affliction ministered to me more than you know."

They both started laughing as they realized that God's ways are not their ways, and the unseen is often the very thing that blesses the most when you see how God uses it.

There were so many people present that Rob had touched in some way. At the time, Rob never gave his acts a second thought and had no idea that people were impacted by them.

There was an elderly woman who Rob helped cross the parking lot on Sundays as he helped in the Church parking lot. There was a man who died in an automobile accident who had attended one of Rob's marriage groups.

A woman who needed financial help because her husband suddenly left her and took all their savings was there, because Rob helped her. There was a store clerk that Rob became friends with over several years. He eventually led him to the Lord. With the clerk, were his wife and their parents who the clerk had led to the Lord as a result of his conversion.

There were business associates and clients that Rob had impacted in some way. Present was a Pastor who was having doubts about his leadership ability as he struggled to minister to a young congregation as he grew older. Rob counseled him from time to time and kept him focused on what God wanted, not on himself. There were several elders who Rob helped when they needed encouragement. The mother of a boy Rob sponsored through World Vision and became a Christian as a result of his generosity. Also present was a camp counselor who had drown as he attempted to swim the lake one evening. Rob had prayed with him about going into full time missions. Each individual had a story about how Rob had that special compassion for each of them and had met them wherever they were. The list went on and on, and as they were introduced and recognized, Rob realized that no riches on earth could ever compare to the reward that he was receiving as he saw the purpose of his life unfold before him.

The room was filled with exotic foods incredible in sight and smell. Rob didn't recognize any of thier varieties. Their color and texture were very different than the fruits and vegetables on earth. They seemed to have a life glow about them that intensified their appeal. The fragrance was like nothing he had ever experienced before. It was if God made their aroma specifically for taste. The closest thing Rob could think of was when Kate would bake his favorite dish in the oven. Rob kept checking to see if it was done as Kate chased him away. Everyone was eating and enjoying the intense flavors as they communicated with each other.

Rob's Dad said, "Try one of these Rob."

As Rob took his first bite, the smell led to a taste that was sweet and delicious. Rob savored the bite and thought that he could eat just this and be completely satisfied. As he took another bite, an angel came and gave him a plate with a variety of fruits cut into pieces for easy consumption. Rob took the plate and thanked the angel mentally. It wasn't difficult as Rob had thought to communicate without speaking. He realized that the senses intensified as the flavors were not interrupted by speech as they ate. Each fruit had a unique consistency and flavor that seemed to melt on his pallet. How wonderful it was to enjoy the endless varieties of food that were before him.

Jesus told Rob that it would be better if He left him with his guests. Jesus knew that if He remained at the banquet, He would be the center of attention, and Jesus wanted Rob to enjoy the fellowship of his family and friends.

Rob thanked Him and asked if he could see Him later.

Jesus said, "You can see me whenever you would like Rob. I can make myself available later after you have fellowshipped here. Please enjoy the banquet, you have much to catch up on, and there is no hurry here."

Then Jesus disappeared.

Rob's son Jason came in and sat across from Rob where Jesus was sitting.

"Hi Dad," he said. "I have so much I want to know about you and mom, and actually being here with you, is much better than seeing you without interaction."

Rob seemed puzzled by the comment. "What do you mean, without interaction?" he asked.

"Jesus would allow me to see what you were doing from time to time on earth. I wanted so much to be able to communicate with you and let you know that I was fine here in the heavenlies. But Jesus would not allow interaction. He said nothing can alter the Father's plan purposes."

Rob laughed and replied, "Yes, I could see how seeing you, or mom and dad, would make my life on earth very complicated. Trying to live my life there and knowing what was happening here in the heavenlies would have been a problem."

The family told stories to Jason about Rob and Art growing up on the river. Rob laughed as they remembered the mischief and fun that were an everyday occurrence in their lives.

Jason told Rob that he and Jesus would go on adventures of their own, and He filled his life with a closeness that replaced the void of Rob not being there. Rob thought how wonderful Jesus was to make a special place in His heart for Jason. He knew that His love was much better than any he was capable of giving.

He also said, "Grandma and Grandpa have taught me so

much, and I've really enjoyed them being here with them." Their relationship has been so fulfilling for me Dad."

"I may seem young to you, but I've been here learning and experiencing many things with Jesus. It is you who have some catching up to do."

Rob decided to spend time at each of the tables to further develop his relationship with each person there. It was amazing how time flew by as he shared with each one individually and as a group. Unlike relationships on earth, there were no selfish motives, no personal agendas, and no pride, as they shared their innermost thoughts. What a joy it was to be where sin had been eliminated, and replaced with God's pure love.

Rob couldn't get over how much food he ate without getting full.

When he asked his mom about it, she laughed and said, "Food here is for enjoyment only, not for sustenance. Have you noticed that you never get hungry either?"

Rob thought for a moment and said, "Now that you mention it, I haven't."

Rob's mom explained, "The food is burned instantly in your new high powered system and has no affect on your energy or power. That comes directly from God Himself."

Rob wasn't sure exactly how that was possible, but knew from the experience that it was true.

Rob felt loved as he enjoyed the banquet and those in attendance. There was so much affinity now that the cares of the world and the lusts of the flesh were removed. Each person connected in perfect harmony with each other. Having his parents and son there completed the experience. He wondered when Kate would join them as he took in the moment. Oh how she would love this, he thought, as everyone laughed and loved one another.

Mansion

Jesus appeared again after Rob had enjoyed time with each one at the banquet. He asked Rob to take a break from the banquet. Jesus wanted to show him something that He had prepared for him. He knew the banquet was just getting started and there would be plenty of time to return to the festivities before it ended.

Rob hugged and kissed his family members, and then thanked everyone for coming to honor him. He told them that he would be back to continue the celebration after his time with the Lord.

"These banquets generally last several days, and you will have plenty of time after we return." Jesus explained.

Rob wasn't surprised when He explained that the festivities would continue as he watched everyone having such a wonderful time.

As they exited the banquet hall, Rob suddenly found himself in front of a tall building adorned with large stones faceted like diamonds each perfectly set into the other. There were angular projections that fit like a puzzle, to create the beautiful pattern that towered above them. The stones were a mixture of metallic looking materials and gems combined, making the light reflect with brilliance. The intricate architectural details were unique and spectacular as light penetrated all the surfaces.

Large openings with balconies were at every angle of the faceted building. Gardens and golden walkways surrounded the structure making it look surreal.

Jesus looked at Rob and said, "Welcome home Rob, this is the mansion I have prepared just for you."

Rob instantly knew that every detail was uniquely made to fulfill the desire of his heart.

Rob exclaimed, "It's so incredible!"

"Come in Rob, you haven't seen it yet," Jesus replied.

Rob was so moved by the generosity and love he felt from Jesus, he said to Him; "You know I am content with the fact that I am here with you. Nothing compares to the joy I have felt while I'm with you."

Jesus looked deep into Rob's eyes and said, "Rob, you know that's what you were created for. These surprises are an expression of Our love for you, and it is my pleasure that you receive these gifts. The wonders that you will experience are to be enjoyed as you would like. You have always given the Glory to God the Father for your blessings. We created you to bring Glory to the Father, and that Glory comes freely from his children whom He loves. That love comes from your free will submission to His authority and Lordship. To do the Father's will is the purest act of unselfishness. That unselfishness makes Him want to bless you abundantly."

Rob paused and then said, "I think I understand. So if I am focused on the desire to praise and glorify the Father, He releases the very things that man in his selfishness seeks for fulfillment and pleasure."

"Exactly, you're beginning to understand it!" said Jesus. "When you understand that We are love, then you know that freedom comes in submission and unselfishness. The opposite is the absence of love, and separation from God the Father. When you seek to do your own will, that is self seeking it removes God the Father from His rightful place as Lord."

They walked up a winding walkway to a large entrance with a magnificent wooden door. As Rob came closer, he could barely believe his eyes. The wooden door was translucent allowing the wood grain to appear all the way through the door. The rich warm golden brown color was fabulous. Intricate carvings framed the door enhancing the translucent dimensions and making its beauty come alive. There was a large golden handle with an inscription carved into its base that read "welcome." As Jesus gently pushed the door open, Rob's eyes went directly to the floor.

The floor was made of the same type of wood and covered the entire surface. The rich glow felt so warm and cozy that it seemed to shrink the size of the massive room. The wood looked as if it were poured, having no seams, and the surface was perfectly smooth. When you looked down at the floor, it looked as if the wood had no end to its depth.

Rob thought about how pale his wood floor, that he laid, in his family room, was compared to this. For several years Rob had dreamed of adding a family room to his cozy little house. The highlight was the warm rich floors that would make the room feel inviting. When Rob finally put the addition on the house, it seemed that all their time was spent in that one room. Family gatherings and special occasions, that were often enjoyed, flooded Rob's mind. Their weekly fellowship group meetings and family gatherings made Rob suddenly realize how he wished everyone was there to see the wonders that the Lord had prepared.

Rob suddenly realized that eventually they would join him, and that the fellowship that he enjoyed back on earth, would be nothing compared to the joy that was here. To think that they would spend eternity here, in this wonderful place, made Rob's emotions soar.

As they entered the mansion, an angel greeted them. Jesus introduced him; "This is Noble your helper." Noble was not as large in stature as many of the other angels and had a friendly appearance. He smiled and seemed pleased to meet Rob.

"I am here Rob," he said, "to meet your needs, if you are in need of anything, please let me know."

Jesus told Rob that Noble would become a close friend and confidant.

Rob looked around the room and inquired as to its purpose. There were seats around the perimeter of the room and clusters of lounge chairs scattered everywhere.

Jesus said, "This is a greeting and fellowship area for guests and friends. People will come and visit, similar to the family gatherings and fellowship groups you hosted back on earth. The clusters are set up to accommodate a dozen people and will allow you to have many intimate group encounters with many of My children. Remember Rob, you will have an eternity to develop and enjoy these relationships. Just think of all the wonderful people you will meet and entertain here in your new home."

Jesus led Rob into a room that was several stories above the fellowship room. The room had two large comfortable lounge chairs. The interior space was small and intimate with chairs facing each other. The room opened up onto a huge balcony overlooking the gardens. From the balcony, you could see various mansions, some larger than others, but each unique and beautiful. They were innumerable and disappeared in the distance. Golden streets and magnificent gardens intertwined together perfectly in every direction.

As Rob looked up, he couldn't believe his eyes. He was amazed that the landscape and buildings extended upward, just as it did outward. It was as if the perspective went out in every direction allowing Rob to view the magnificent city from any angle and direction.

As Rob looked at the sight, Jesus explained, "The city is as high as it is wide. That's why the mansions and palaces have such magnificent views. I have made each one unique, specific to the every individual personality. Each mansion has ministering angels that serve Our children. They were created to minister to you in every way."

Jesus asked Rob to sit in one of the two lounge chairs in the small room. Jesus also sat down, as he looked into Rob's eyes, He said, "Rob, this is our special place where you and I will meet as often as you would like. I have so much to tell you, and I'm sure you have many questions to ask Me as well."

The intimacy felt by Rob was indescribable. He could sit there indefinitely listening to Jesus.

Then Jesus said, "Here in Heaven, sin does not exist, therefore perfect intimacy can be experienced not only between you and I, but also with others. That is why there is no marriage here. The more you know Me Rob, the deeper your understanding will become, and the closer you will feel toward Me. That is also true as you get to know the many people here, and more so, with your family. You are all the Father's children and therefore you are all family. Everyone here is an heir and a child of God, therefore, you will inherit all that the Father has and dwell in His presence. The material wonders are not the real riches Rob. The richer rewards are found in the joy that comes from being where the Father is and in a relationship with Him and His other children."

Rob asked Jesus why he hadn't seen any bedrooms in the mansion. "Rob," Jesus said, "There are no bedrooms, because there is no need for rest here. Everything receives its energy and power from the Father, and not from the substances you consume. Therefore, bedrooms are replaced with rooms for fellowship, rooms for enjoyment, and gathering rooms for festivities, to entertain and enjoy one another. Life here is simple because the sin that created the humanity's separation has been removed. All things have been perfected. Your uniqueness will be used to rule over much of Our creation. Later, you will learn your role in Our plan."

Jesus showed Rob areas with fountains and pools filled with shimmering water. The mansion seemed to cascade from one area to another on multiple levels. Each area was created to enhance and accommodate intimate fellowship. Some of the settings created celebratory moods while others a sense of singular intimacy. The colors, the materials used, the seating areas, the fountains, pools, balconies, gardens, flowers, and exotic plants all combined to make this place Rob's own personal place of intimacy.

Jesus took Rob to the top level of his new home, to a lovely garden terrace with exotic plants unlike anything he had ever seen on earth. Rich vibrant colors surrounded him. In the center of the terrace was a single chair made of gold and adorned with magnificent jewels. It was like a throne but had soft tapestry at an angle to provide a relaxed seating position for comfort and relaxation.

There was a single book sitting in the center of a small table in front of the throne. Rob asked Jesus to explain this place to him.

Jesus picked up the book and handed it to Rob. "Sit," he said, "open the book."

Rob sat down and as he looked at the book, he could see that it was a Bible. The binding was beautiful and soft and in golden letters on the front it read, "The Living Word". Rob slowly opened the book, and as he read from Genesis, the words actually became visual making the event play out exactly as it happened. How exciting it was to actually see the events as they really happened.

He wondered if the future events that were professed would also be visible, and as he turned to the book of Revelation, the events played out just as they did when he viewed the past.

As Rob looked up at Jesus smiling, he remembered his daily quiet times that he had each day in the Bible, trying to comprehend the Scriptures. As Rob grew older, his desire to understand and know more was the highlight of his day.

Jesus said, "Rob, your desire to know Me, My Father, and to let the Holy Spirit work in your life, was counted as righteousness to you. As a reward for your obedience and submission, I am giving you this Book for your good pleasure and understanding. The book will provide understanding and wisdom for your eternal journey."

Rob asked, "My eternal journey?"

Jesus answered, "Yes, your short life on earth was masked by the pull of your flesh, by principalities of darkness unseen, and by the world. You will continue to spend time here in the Living Word. Your understanding will grow exponentially as you understand Our work, love, and relationship that will bring you closer to Us. This special place is my favorite gift to you."

Rob fell to his knees and said, "I am so undeserving of this Lord."

"Arise Rob, you are loved, and it is my good pleasure to give these things to you."

Hell

Art was confused, as he saw his daughter asking the doctor to take him off life support. He seemed to be hovering above her and over his own battered body lying on the hospital bed. The only thing Art could remember was the truck crashing into him. The pain that accompanied the impact and then the few seconds of consciousness was so intense that he wished he would die. Then, in the next moment, he was taken away and found himself in total darkness.

As he looked up from where he was lying, all he could see was blackness. The realization that he must be dead gripped him as he wondered where he was and why there was no light.

The stench gagged him as he tried to pull himself up. He was so weak that every movement seemed to drain him of any remaining energy. He asked himself if this was a dream or if it was real. When he finally got himself to a sitting position, he could make out a faint shadow of what seemed to be a chamber with an iron gate that enclosed an entrance.

While his eyes adjusted to the blackness of the walls seemed to move invoking a fear like he had never felt before. Off in the distance he could see fire which allowed him to see shadows.

Then Art looked up, and he could see the silhouette of a large morbid creature that was powerful and hideous. The creature cursed at him and exclaimed "Ahh another human" as he reached down and threw Art against the wall. Art was helpless and couldn't even begin to protect himself. As his head slammed against the stone wall, he felt a pulsating pain that made him buckle over. He thought momentarily that he wished he were dead, but then realized that he was, at least physically. He wanted so much for the whole experience to end that he shrieked with agony. When he screamed, it seemed to please the creature, and he smashed his face into the stone wall.

The creature was chained to the stone wall limiting his movements. Art knew if he could only move away from the wall, that he would be out of the reach of the creature.

Thoughts of him not being able to escape from the creature and this awful place consumed him and intensified his fear. Where was he? Was this punishment for his disbelief in God, or, was it just a horrid dream? He told himself to wake up hoping it was just a dream. As the moments passed he realized that it wasn't a dream, and the fear intensified.

He knew that he had no ability to control his situation. For Art, this was one of the first times that he didn't feel in control and felt completely helpless. He screamed at the creature to stay away, but as he was screaming, the creature ripped at his chest and rammed his fist into his face. He thought how could he endure such a blow and yet live. Repeatedly, the creature attacked him.

Each time he tried to move away from the wall where the creature was chained the creature threw him against the wall keeping him captive.

Art never experienced fear like this, and the more he tried to escape, the weaker he felt. Pain ripped his body and he agonized over the intensity of each blow. He wondered how long he could endure this torture? He cried for relief, but none came. He screamed for mercy, and there was no mercy.

As he looked down at his body, he could see that he was naked. The fact that his clothes were removed made him feel even more vulnerable. His body was his, but seemed to have a translucency that wasn't quite flesh, but wasn't spirit either. His mind raced wondering how he could escape and find something to cover his nakedness. But deep inside, he knew there would be no escape, or covering, from this evil place. Every thought seemed to grip his inner most soul and leave him depleted. The blows should have ripped his body apart, but there was no blood, only pain.

The heat and dryness made each breath almost impossible to take. The smell was the most retched odor he had ever encountered and made him nauseous. It was if death was everywhere mixed with a sulfur smell. The smoldering surface spewed a noxious smoke and made everything barely visible.

As he looked up, he could see the silhouette of slimy worms crawling everywhere. His mind panicking as he tried to figure out how he could escape from the place, but deep down, he knew there was no escape.

Evil permeated the air and made Art feel angry. As his anger increased, Art cursed at the creature and asked him to kill him.

The creature snarled, and said, "I would love to kill you, but you humans won't die." He reached down and threw Art into the iron bars.

This place was so terrible and he knew that Art must be in Hell. He felt so alone and wondered how long he would be there. Every time Art tried to get to his feet the creature would slam him down. Art couldn't imagine that there would really be a place like this, and regrets made him wish he would have been more receptive to his brother's warnings about Hell. Rob had told Art that Hell was a real place and that it was far worse, than what anyone could imagine.

Art began cursing at God saying; "How could you do this to me!" As his anger increased he could feel the hatred rise up and permeate his soul.

The presence of God was absent from this place and evil was contagious like a disease. Everything was rotting, and the stench of death was overwhelming. It seemed like an eternity had passed when the cell door opened and Art was summoned into the darkness. As the door opened he could see a pathway and the glow of fire a long distance off. Art struggled, but eventually made it to his feet and exited the cell as fast as he could.

At first Art was glad to get out of the cell and away from the awful creature, but then fear began to set in that where he was headed, might be even worse.

Outside of the cell was even more terrifying than what was experienced inside the cell with the creature. Everywhere he looked were horrific creatures chained to the walls. Smoke was spewing up from the empty space that was between him and the glowing fire off in the distance. He could see the silhouettes of others heading toward the fire and knew that he too must go there as well.

Each step he took was painful and exhausting. It was as if the life was being sucked out of him. Screaming demons were cursing God. There were people moving toward the fire from every direction. The smell of rotting flesh and the sight of consuming worms was more than he could bare.

Art fell to his knees and pleaded that he would be taken from this place. He pleaded for mercy; but none came, he cried out for death; but death did not come, he offered God a deal that if he removed him, he would do whatever God wanted. But then he realized it was too late. Art's chance for mercy and forgiveness was squandered by his pride while he lived a decadent and self-absorbed life on earth. He couldn't believe that his life had ended so abruptly. Then he started blaming God and lashing out at God, for putting him in Hell. As he moved along, his spirit became like the creatures chained to the walls. As he too cursed God, the pain, the heat, and the agony of the situation became greater and greater.

Art came to a passageway that led into a lake of fire. He was now being pushed along by a sea of people who were headed toward the fire as well. The heat became so intense that his feet felt like they were going to burst into flames. As he looked down, the pathway was actually glowing from the heat. The agony of the heat was so painful that all Art could do was scream. He tried to jump to free his feet from the intense pain, but he didn't have enough energy to lift his feet off the surface.

As he entered the large abyss he could see small pits that appeared to be made to hold individual souls. Many of them were filled, and the screams and agony of the souls in them was deafening. Screams, pleading for the pain and suffering to end seemed to expose the evil in each soul as they gnashed their teeth and cursed God. Their agony intensified their hatred as their suffering continued. The evil in their hearts brought out the worst in them.

Art wondered if he would be cast into the large lake of fire, or if he too would be put into a pit specifically made for him. It seemed to him that the pain inflicted upon each soul was different.

He wondered how bad his fate would be, considering that he really didn't care about, or give any consideration for anything, or anyone but himself. His motto was if it felt good, do it. Art had left a wake of relationships ruined in his path and his lifestyle was absent of any consideration for others on earth. His arrogance had no bounds and as he gained the riches of the world he isolated himself of any meaningful relationships.

Even Art's family had made no impact upon his attitude or his actions. As the years went by, his heart became absent of any compassion or love for anyone. Art filled his life with the seeking of pleasures. The self-seeking desires consumed his private life as he lusted after women and sought increasing amounts of alcohol, drugs, and sexual additions. The more he tried to satisfy his lusts and desires, the emptier he became inside. The momentary pleasure always fleeted and led to an increasing frequency of lustful consumption. But deep inside, Art was empty, lonely, and depressed. His indulgences then turned to anger as he felt sorry for himself, because he felt used by others, who sought after his wealth.

He entered the large gulf of fire that seemed to extend as far as he could see. Once again he could only think of how unfair this was and that he didn't deserve this punishment. His delusion of himself was truly blinded by his outrageous pride and the lusts of the world.

Bitterness had replaced any form of love in his heart, and he believed that everyone he knew was using him in some way. The distortion of his soul was reflected in how he viewed others including his family. The pain and suffering were simply a consequence of what his life was like while he was alive on earth. Hell brought out the evil that was subdued while Art was alive. His darkened heart was now exaggerated to its fullest extent.

Art struggled to walk further, but the fear of one of the horrific creatures getting to him kept him moving. As the creatures reached out trying to rip him to pieces, he cowered and felt like a fly waiting to be swatted by the gigantic creatures. As he looked at them, he realized they were all huge as compared to him. Each one had varied appearances and features. They seemed to manifest the unique evil nature that each one possessed.

Their hatred for humans had no bounds, and as they tried to get to them. The chains restricted their reach and confined their ability to move. Every so often one of them would connect with a human sending them to the floor in pain. When this happened it seemed to give them pleasure knowing that they caused suffering by the blow of their hand.

Cursing blasphemies at God and his creation seemed to be their only desire. They called out to Satan to rescue them from their torment and to destroy God. Their appearance became more evil and distorted as they cursed and blasphemed God's name. As Art stood waiting for the next torture, he could see other creatures that didn't yet have their grotesque appearance being chained to the walls. Their appearance would gradually change as they screamed with hatred. Art wondered if it was happening to him as his hatred increased.

Suddenly, Art was in a small pit. It was about ten feet in diameter and the flames and smoke made him shriek with pain. His entire body felt as if it were burning and the smell of burning flesh permeated the space. He tried to climb out but the weakness and pain made it impossible to climb the slimy wall that now surrounded him. His mouth was so dry that even screaming made his lips and tongue sticky and fused together. If only he could get some water to quench his thirst. He then cried out for relief. The more he struggled to escape, the more intense the fire became. If only he had a drink of water, he thought, he would be satisfied.

Art was so tired, but the pain prevented him from resting. The energy he did possess was consumed by the cries and blasphemies that were unending. Smoke filled the pit making him choke as the toxic fumes filled his lungs. As he sat there gnashing his teeth, he noticed worms all over his body. He tried to rub them off, but the pain just in touching his skin was more than he could bear.

All thoughts of anything other than his pain and agony were absent. His eternity now set, he was now the product of his life without God. His destiny was now and forever more, a product of God's wrath. The isolation and finality of his situation gripped him as he fell to his knees pleading for help. Art watched others fill the endless pits that stretched out as far as he could see. The number of souls there were innumerable.

Art screamed for God to remove him from his agony.

The creatures laughed at him and said, "Forget about God, pray that Satan will come and release us you fool."

They shouted blasphemies at the Lord and prayed to their lord, who is Satan.

As Art anguished and cried for relief, the ugliness within him again resurfaced as he cursed God and yelled, "I don't deserve this! Kill me! If there is a God, kill me!"

All the creatures laughed at him as they reveled in his anguish. Then the pain gripped him again, and all he could do was scream in agony, forever.

Why

"Rob," Jesus said, as he reached for Rob's arm, "I have something I need to tell you."

Rob seemed puzzled by the tone and the gesture sensing that it wasn't going to be good news.

"Your brother died in an automobile accident the day after you arrived here. I'm afraid that you won't be seeing him again."

Rob instantly knew that Art was in Hell. Then Rob remembered the letter.

"Did Art receive my letter?" Rob asked.

"No Rob, the letter arrived the day after he died."

Rob was disturbed by the fact that he had spent so much of his time in his final days writing and rewriting that letter, that it was all for nothing.

Jesus knew that Rob felt cheated by the timing of the events and the remorse he felt knowing his brother was eternally damned.

Rob looked at Jesus and said, "Why?"

Jesus gently replied, "Rob, I know how hard it must be right now for you. Your feelings toward your brother were strong and your attempts to reach him recognizing that his path was leading toward eternal death, grieves me even more than it does you. Remember Rob, I am omniscient, and even if the letter had reached him before his death, he would not have changed his views. Art's pride much like Lucifer's, darkened his outlook and hardened his heart. Down deep, Art was empty and angry. His pursuit of power and money made him increasingly dead to any goodness in his heart. That is the trap and the lie of the physical world ruled by Satan."

"All of Art's money and power couldn't prevent his death. He believed that he would live to a ripe old age. His obsession with his health and excellent physical condition made him think that death was something to think about much later in life. Many deceive themselves thinking that they are in total control of their future. Their pride and arrogance are ultimately their demise. As they are consumed into the lusts of the eyes and the pride of life, the desire to know God is veiled by their sins. Their increasing desire for more, makes it impossible to be enlightened with the truth. Eventually we must give them over to their own lusts and abandon the pursuit, because we know it is futile. Sometimes we allow adversity to bring them to their knees. But often times, we know that it will not change the path that they are on."

"Rob I came to the earth to testify to the truth. That truth is only obtained in Me, through Me, and of Me. It is my written word laid before the foundation of time, where man has the choice to accept Me or reject Me. The majority of mankind rejects the truth for a lie. It is the deceitfulness of the world, the lust of the eyes, and the weakness of the flesh that blinds mankind to accept the lies of Satan and his world order. When I came to earth and gave Myself up for humanity, a new choice was given to everyone. My sacrifice allowed them an escape from eternal punishment and separation from God. Even with that opportunity, many have chosen the darkness offered through the lies of Satan. They sell their eternal existence in paradise for the momentary pleasure of their lustful hearts. I am saddened by the deception that rules their hearts and minds."

Jesus took Rob's arm again and this time had an uplifting expression of encouragement. "I know your brother's fate saddens you as it does s. The letter that you sent to Art reached receptive ears as it was read by Kate at your memorial service. Moreover, it was read by Art's daughter Courtney who received My gift of salvation, and then by many as she read it at Art's memorial service."

Rob looked surprised, and asked, "You mean Art's daughter accepted your gift of eternal life because of my letter?"

"Yes, Rob," He replied, "Not only did Courtney come to faith but also her mother, as well as many prominent businessmen, as she read your letter at the memorial service. Kate also read your letter at your own memorial service, where many of your clients and old classmates were also in attendance. In all forty-six souls were saved by your letter at the two memorial services."

Jesus continued, "It might be helpful for you to look ahead and realize the eternal impact that your letter will have on all of humankind. Your letter transformed Courtney's life. She will devote her life's work to defending and working with legal cases where the Word of God is being denied and or restrained. Her non-profit ministry will reach many for the gospel. The wealth that Art accumulated will be used to reach countless souls for the Kingdom. Her foundation will impact governments and multitudes of people worldwide."

"Some of the prominent businessmen that were there at Art's memorial service were billionaires, and several turned to Me for salvation. They will also form foundations where their money will be used for the funding of Church plants worldwide. Their fortunes will provide millions of dollars for churches and will reach over one million souls before it's over."

"That's not all Rob," Jesus interjected again, "Kate decided to post your letter on the internet. That letter has been read by several hundred thousand people in 30 different countries worldwide. Your letter has prompted thousands of people to accept salvation by believing in Me."

Rob was overwhelmed by what Jesus had just revealed to him. "I'm in shock," Rob exclaimed, "and even though my effort had no impact on Art's life, it was used by You for the greater good."

He now understood how God makes all things work together for good for those who love him. It was a bittersweet moment, realizing that his brother, whom he dearly loved, was in hell, but that many had and would receive eternal life. Rob also knew how much more it grieves God, who has a perfect love, that Art chose his own way.

Rob asked Jesus, "Does this type of thing happen often?"

Jesus smiled and said, "More than you think it's the little things that set activities in motion that impact lives. These events, that are all intertwined, are invisibly working behind the scenes and converting souls. It's the faithful few like you that do God's work for the Kingdom. It is ultimately love in its various forms that have the real impact in bringing humankind to salvation."

"As a result of your faithfulness and in service for the kingdom, you will meet a multitude of people who you helped toward salvation. Their gratitude will be part of your eternal reward. These relationships will grow and prosper as you fellowship and share eternity together."

Rob realized that his mom and dad would know about Art by now and he knew how they would be feeling.

Jesus was prepared for the moment and told Rob that his mom and dad were waiting for him downstairs in one of the gathering rooms.

Jesus said, "I'll let you have some time with your family. I know your mom would like to see you, she took the news pretty hard."

Rob replied, "Thank you for helping me see that there is a greater purpose in this tragedy."

In an instant, Jesus was gone and Rob was standing in front of his mom.

As he appeared, Rob's mom pulled him in for a long hug. She looked into his eyes and knew that they shared a sorrow, that only they could have, because of their close relationship.

She said, "I know how close you two were growing up. As Art grew apart from our family, I could see the changes that the power and wealth brought to him. I can't help but wonder if there was something I could have done to bring him back into our family."

 Mom," Rob replied, "You did everything and more to make Art feel loved and part of the family. It was his choice to shut us out, and yes, I do miss the close relationship we enjoyed as children, but I couldn't make him accept Christ."

Rob's dad came and hugged them both as they asked the Lord to give them strength. Jesus is also grieving over Art, He knew that his fate could not be altered and his choices and rejection of Him was necessary for the overall good that it produced. How awful it must be to grieve over each of His creations who are lost into darkness. It helped them knowing that the rest of the family would one day be with them there in the glory of the Lord.

Rob's dad had traveled to New York several years earlier to try and talk to Art. He was surprised, when Art's business meetings took precedence over spending time with him. After chasing after Art for three days, his dad was only able to have one short dinner with him. His dinner ended abruptly, as Art received a call from his attorney regarding a deal that was pending. Art told his Dad that he did not have the time to see him and that he really didn't want to hear about the Jesus stuff anyway. He was hurt knowing that, Art didn't care about anyone but himself.

Rob's mom finally said, "We all tried our best. Art made his own choices and none of us could stop him from his demise. We must continue to keep our perspective and trust in our Father, for it is His will that really matters. When I think of how much, we that know Him have been blessed it takes away all the sadness. We must move past this and embrace the joy here in Heaven."

Rob was saddened by the thought of Art and others being separated from the wonderful relationship that was available for those who make Jesus their Lord. He needed time to process the reality of a world where the majority of the people have no idea how critical their choices are during their short life on earth. As much as he was loving the experience of heaven, it was hard not to think about what it must be like where God is absent.

Jesus embraced Rob and said, "We have given mankind many obvious opportunities and provided a supernatural desire to develop a personal relationship with Us. Our good desire is to reach each of Our children to receive what We have made available. If only they weren't so hard-hearted. The deceit of the world is seductive. The gospel is foolishness to those who are perishing. The simplicity of salvation often confounds the wise, and is impossible for much of those in the world to accept."

"They all know in their heart of hearts the truth. They refuse to accept it because they refuse to give up control of the sins that they covet. It ultimately comes down to their own worldly wisdom rather than God's wisdom. Because salvation comes at a cost, they suppress the truth. Placing God as their Lord repels their desire to receive salvation."

Angels and Demons

After learning about Art's fate, Rob wondered why sin first entered the world and why Satan would deceive humans. He wondered why after seeing angels in this wonderful place, they would rebel against God and then hate mankind.

Rob seemed surprised when Jesus said, "So you want to know more about Lucifer and what happened to him? Well, you probably know that We created the angelic hosts to glorify Us. They were created before man, and as you can see, they are spirit beings. We created a variety of angels for differing functions and hierarchal positions, in the Heavenly realm. They, like mankind, are each individual in personality and giftedness. No one angel is like another."

"Lucifer, or Satan (the deceiver), was Our most magnificent creation. His beauty and power surpassed all the other angels. He was perfect in every way and his intellect was beyond all other creation. We clothed him with jewels and his splendor was majestic. His beauty was radiant and perfect. Lucifer dazzled with brilliance, appearing as light, and was the head cherubim before the Father's throne."

"We gave angels free will, just as we did with human kind. Lucifer was found to have deceit in his heart and chose to glorify himself rather than the Father. Because We created him to have many of the attributes that We possess, he became proud and exalted himself. His pride grew as he ruled the Heavenly host. Soon he deceived himself in thinking that he could be equal or above Us. Lucifer saw that many angels bowed before him and obeyed his every command. His lust for more power grew and eventually made him believe that he was also a god. His desire to be worshipped prevented him from the relationship that he was created for with Us. Lucifer's pride made him an enemy of God, as he sought to rule over all creation."

Rob asked, "Why are there so many types of angels here?"

Jesus replied, "Think about it Rob, since the angels are spiritual creations that are capable of manifesting themselves in differing forms, they take on the form that compliments their function. Angelic warriors will take on the form that allows them to execute the Father's will, through them, by suppressing evil. That's why, as an example, Reveal, your guardian angel, is a formidable spirit that manifests himself as a loving guardian."

Jesus further explained, "A cherub that guards against the principalities of Satan and his followers will be a fearsome warrior that is supremely powerful. A messenger will take on the form much like a man because their purpose is delivering God's instruction and guidance. The cherubs that are before our throne reveal Our holiness and glory. We have created an unlimited variety of manifestations for their specific purposes."

"Lucifer was cast down to earth along with all of his devoted followers, about a third of all the angels. God allowed limited access to His throne and suppressed his powers, while allowing Lucifer to roam the earth. With hearts filled with deceit and self righteousness, they became increasingly evil and were banned from free access to the Father."

"Satan attacks and accuses those who have made Me Lord as he tries to remove their imputed righteousness by presenting their sins before the Father. His deceit has no bounds, and he continues to deceive humans as he did Eve, in the Garden of Eden. He knows that he has a limited time before he is cast into the lake of fire. He desires to take all of human kind with him if he can."

"To show Our power and Our glory, pt was necessary to change the original order of angels. They were created above humankind, but when Lucifer deceived Eve and sin entered mankind, it was necessary to redeem mankind from Our judgment and wrath."

"Atonement for sins past, present, and future, had to be made in order for a fallen creation to come before the Father, the Son, and the Holy Spirit. That is why I came to the earth as a man, and then allowed My own suffering and death. That was the only way We could redeem mankind. We are Holy, therefore nothing unholy may exist in Our presence. Only by sacrifice of blood leading to physical death can sin be forgiven."

Jesus explained, "Lucifer's defeat came when I defeated death and was resurrected from the grave. My coming to earth and becoming a man, placed redeemed mankind higher than the angels in both position and power. My sacrifice atoned for the sins of those who have embraced and believed in Me. I am the only way to the access of Our presence and this Holy place. Those that choose to reject My atoning gift will suffer forever in Hades and the bottomless pit which is Hell."

"Rob," Jesus said, "I know that you sought Me and believed in Me without fully understanding the battle that take place in the heavenly realm over human kind. Remember, wide is the path that leads to destruction and narrow is the way to salvation. Our great love for Our human creation, allowed Us to make a way for those who deserve separation and death from God, to access the relationship that was intended."

"Separation from Us, removes all that is good. Being with Us, accesses all that is good. The forces that work outside the physical world are powerful and real. These dimensions where principalities and powers are unseen by mankind, are warring against each other and are ever present. This spiritual war is waged by Satan and his followers, and their goal is to deceive people and damn them forever."

"Satan's beauty that was manifested by God the Father turned into the personification of evil apart from the Father. His beauty transformed into a reflection of what he is, a serpent. His seven heads as a cherub turned into seven heads of wickedness. This beast-like transformation made Lucifer hate God the Father. His inner ugliness apart from God is increasingly growing as the wickedness in his heart also intensifies. Likewise, his followers also are a reflection of the evil in their hearts. Satan seeks to destroy all that We created because he knows his time is limited and his fate eternally damned. In his arrogance he still believes that somehow he can defeat the Father and rule the heavenly realm."

"Michael, who was second in command and almost as magnificent as Lucifer, is now the reigning cherub in the heavenly realm. His power was, and is, increasing, while Lucifer's is decreasing."

"The powers given Michael will be revealed at My return, when the elect will rise from the grave and gather in the heavenly realm. The Father utilizes the angelic multitudes specific to their purpose. They live to do the will of the Father. He has put it in their hearts to do what pleases Him. This brings them ultimate joy and satisfaction."

"It is only the angels warring in the spiritual dimension that protects human kind against the wrath of Satan and his followers. Our love for all human souls has kept the balance, allowing each person a choice for all those who would receive the free gift of salvation for all who believe."

"Rob, you have been protected by an army of angels that watched over you. When you accepted my free gift of salvation by faith and believed in me, there was rejoicing throughout the heavenly, over you. You didn't know that you had an army of angels celebrating over your salvation, did you? We rejoiced at your choice Rob, just as We do with all whose name is written in the book of life."

Rob intellectually understood most of these truths, but as Jesus spoke, a supernatural spiritual understanding filled him. He knew God loved him, but now he finally understood how much he loves every person. His love has no bounds, and His sacrifice for mankind is beyond understanding. How selfish and prideful Rob felt as Jesus explained His love for all humans. His desire that all would believe and embrace Him and accept His free gift is so unlike the nature of the human race; only God could and would love like that.

"You speak of warfare in the Spiritual realm, in what ways?" Rob asked.

"Rob, you are in a dimension that is invisible to the physical world. All that you are experiencing here exists in dimensions outside the physical three dimensional space that is known in the physical world. That's why time for Us is meaningless. We are able to make today, tomorrow, and yesterday appear at Our will. This dimension is a different time and space than the one that you experienced on earth."

"Remember when you were reading the Living Word and you could see what would happen in the future?"

"Yes," Rob replied. "It was incredible."

Jesus explained, "That's because everything in the future, everything that happened in the past, is visible presently to Us. You always experienced time as a passing thing on earth that had a beginning, a present tense, and a future tense. In reality, it is a single dimension that only is seen in a physical sense. There are many other dimensions that exist that were hidden from you until now. The dimensions of time are infinite, and therefore relative to the space you occupy."

Rob looked puzzled for a moment and then seemed to have an epiphany.

"So that's why I can transport myself to another space at will?"

Jesus replied, "Exactly Rob, time becomes a space that We control and make visible, and that space can be occupied at will by Me. That's how angels are able to travel back and forth between the physical dimension and the spiritual dimension."

So Rob asked, "Is it possible to travel the universe?"

Jesus smiled and said, "Absolutely, let me explain, because this is where it's gets tricky. Yes, you can go there in a spiritual dimension, but not in the physical dimension."

Jesus further explained, "When you receive your glorified body at the rapture, then you will be able to move from both the physical and the spiritual realm at will."

Rob asked why Jesus didn't just give humans their transfigured bodies as soon as they entered heaven.

"Good question Rob," Jesus replied, "the reason that you have a temporary soul body is because access to the physical world, where family and friends exist, would be too difficult for humans to resist. They would desire the intercession into the affairs of the physical realm. That intervention, and the altering of man's free will and destiny, would complicate God's ultimate plan. Remember that it is God the Father's will that no man should perish, but the choice must be made entirely by each individual. God gave man His Holy Scripture and His creation as a testimony, so that mankind is without excuse. Imagine how life would be confused on earth if the physically diseased appeared resurrected before the living."

Jesus revealed that many of Lucifer's followers had been cast and chained within hell. Their demonic activities prior to the flood, when they procreated with humans, put them there as they tried to seduce and destroy God's elect. Their hatred and lust to destroy all good, forced Us to chain them in Hades, the abyss. In their confinement, their hatred continues to grow. Their blasphemies and increasing hatred makes their torture even more severe, and their suffering more extreme. As they conspire and devise ways to escape, the realization of the futility in their pursuit makes them seek to destroy the lost human souls that are there.

"Rob," Jesus said, "The body that you have now, is the inner soul of a more powerful and multi-dimensional body to come. Your resurrected transfigured body that you will receive at the resurrection of the elect will have the ability to move through all dimensions, both physical and spiritual. You will be able to go through physical space as well as from dimension to dimension including time dimensions. When your resurrected body is transfigured, you will enjoy the ability to move outside of heaven and into the entire universe that was created for the Father's redeemed children. That is why you have been chosen to rule with us, throughout the universe forever."

The Trinity

Rob still pondered what he had learned and how it all fit together. There were so many aspects of God in Their Personhood that were unclear in Rob's mind. Rob asked Jesus if he could spend some time with him to explain some thoughts that he had.

Jesus replied, "You mean mysteries?"

Rob said, "Yes, I have been confused and uncertain about many things I've read in the Bible, things that I've always wondered about."

Jesus put his hand on his shoulder, and tenderly said, "Sure Rob, I am available whenever you would like."

"Rob," Jesus said, "I would suggest that you get back to your banquet, everyone is waiting to spend more time with you. Remember Rob, there are no deadlines or time constraints here, you literally have forever."

Rob replied, "I know, but there is so much to learn and being with you is so incredible that it's hard to believe it's really happening to me. I want to know so many things. I'm sorry that I'm so intent on understanding these things."

Jesus smiled and as he looked tenderly at Rob said, "Everyone, when they first get here, seek a fundamental understanding of Our mysteries that were hidden from them on earth."

When Rob returned to the banquet, he heard beautiful music playing as he entered the room. The sound was soothing and peaceful. An instrument was played that produced a sound that was beautiful and made Rob feel as if it was specifically made to appeal to him. As he was drawn toward the music, he saw that the instrument looked similar to a large harp, but it was a sound uniquely it's own.

Rob asked his dad, "Who is the musician?"

Rob's dad told him that it was Johann Sebastian Bach, the great composer. His dad then explained that his passion is playing at banquets like this one. He plays over 100 instruments and composes music for each.

"Rob, I've become a close friend of his, and he knew that Jesus was having a banquet for you, so he asked Jesus to pick the music that you would love."

Rob thanked Johann for playing and asked if he would join them at his table, so he could learn more about his music.

"Do you prefer to be called Johann?" Rob asked.

Johann smiled and said, "Yes Rob, my friends call me Johann. Then he asked, "How do you like the music?"

Rob replied, "Johann, I've never heard anything quite so soothing and pleasant to my ear. Your music was more appealing to me than any music I've ever experienced with the exception of course, of the music that I heard at the throne of God. Both are indescribable and wonderful beyond imagination."

"Jesus picked the instrument and the compositions for this banquet." he replied. "He knows the perfect combination for each person's individual tastes. He has me compose music for everyone who arrives here. I had the privilege of composing this music for you."

"How long have you been here?" asked Rob.

Johann laughed and replied, "Give or take a few centuries, but who's counting! I love these banquets because each individual discovers their own perfect music style. My soul connects with theirs, as they listen to their own individually crafted music. Jesus helps me craft songs for everyone. Can I continue to play a few songs for you now?" He asked.

Rob could see that Johann's joy came from the music he created and played.

The songs allowed Rob to disconnect from the activities and festivities of the banquet. The music reached deep into his soul and produced a blissful joy that overwhelmed him as he listened. As Johann looked at Rob, he could see that the music penetrated him in a way that he had never experienced before. Johann smiled and was filled with the Spirit, as the melodies filled the air.

After several hours of soothing music, Johann came over and asked Rob if he could change to a different type of music.

Rob laughed and said, "Sure, what are you going to play?"

Johann looked at Rob's dad and said, "Your dad's favorite."

Johann took out a strange futuristic looking instrument.

Rob's dad laughed and said to Rob, "He's playing my audio-flux that I created."

Rob looked surprised and asked. "I didn't know you were musical?"

His dad smiled and said, "Here, all things are possible."

Johann started moving his hands over a glowing keyboard. As he moved his hands over the instrument, a variety of sounds emerged and filled the air. The motion that Johann made was graceful, complex, and the sounds were as well. The music was rhythmic and catchy, penetrating deep within Rob's soul.

Rob's mom and dad got up and began dancing. They laughed like little children as they rhythmically danced to the music. Rob couldn't believe how much fun everyone was having.

Two Ways to an End

When Rob's dad returned from dancing, he said. "Rob, many of the instruments Johann played were designed and created by me. Johann and I have worked on new music concepts, and as you can see Rob, they are new and unique."

"Dad, I'm amazed by this new music, it's so joyous and freeing," Rob replied, "I couldn't stop tapping to the rhythm."

The angels attended to every need as they served everyone various cut fruits, vegetables, and other exotic foods. The flavors were incredible and every bite was savored as Rob ate the food. As he ate, he wondered why he didn't feel full. The sensation was strange considering he consumed a sizable amount of food. Guests came and went, for several days, as there was no end to the stories and experiences they all shared with Rob. He now understood how these banquets could go on for weeks. The reality that time here is never an issue because there are no deadlines, no need for rest, and the need to keep track of time is unnecessary. Rob craved more fellowship with Jesus and asked his guests if they would excuse him from the banquet because he wanted to spend some time with the Lord. They all understood, knowing Rob would have many questions for Jesus.

Rob left the banquet hall and as he looked down the golden street, he realized that he knew exactly where he was, and how to get to his home. As he focused on his home, he suddenly found himself there. Somehow, he had transported himself back to his mansion. He opened the door and went directly to the room that Jesus created for their fellowship. When he entered the room, Jesus was sitting there waiting for Rob.

"I hope you haven't been waiting long," Rob said.

"No, I just sat down Rob," Jesus replied.

"I knew that you wanted to ask me some questions."

"How did you know that?" Rob asked, but then he realized that Jesus was omniscient and knows everything, even the things that have not happened yet.

"Jesus" Rob asked, "I've always wondered about the Trinity. When I came before the throne, it was as if You, the Father, and the Holy Spirit were One. I was before all three of You, but you were One. It's difficult for me to grasp how You, the Father and the Holy Spirit are all one God even though I saw and experienced it myself. As I studied the Scriptures, it revealed that there is only one true God, but I can see that You, the Father and the Holy Spirit are three separate Persons. How can that be?"

Jesus smiled and said, "This concept is probably one of the most difficult for you to fully understand in human terms. The concept of Our wholeness, yet separateness, is only understood supernaturally. Just as man was created with a body, soul, and spirit, in the image of God, so too, We are one God having three separate personhoods."

"Rob," Jesus explained, "Remember, here there are dimensions that in the physical world are unseen by mankind. As an illustration, imagine that the Father, Myself, and the Holy Spirit are three distinct dimensions of the same Object. That Object is what you call God. Because we transcend beyond the universe and the understanding of all created things, We reveal Ourselves through Our personhood, in order that we might be known. Our triune nature allows perfect relationship within Us."

"We are in fact, unknowable, because We are! Therefore, for you to understand Our attributes and then apply these attributes toward Us and others, We revealed the triune relationship that exists within Us so that you would be able to have a relationship with Us. Without the Holy Spirit living within you, spiritual understanding of Us would be impossable. If I hadn't become a man and died and reconciled your unrighteousness, you would not be able to see Us."

"Rob, I know this is taxing the limits of your understanding, but if you understand that nothing exists without Us, then you also understand that We cannot be fully understood because a creation can not fully understand the creator."

"Let me give you an example Rob."

"Remember when you brought your dog, Ginger, home for Kate?"

"Sure," Rob replied.

"You picked her, because you thought she was the smartest dog you had ever seen. She understood tricks and commands quickly, but her capacity had its limits. So, would you expect that little dog to understand and explain the theory of gravity, and how it affects her life? Her ability to have an understanding far beyond her capacity doesn't diminish your love for her, but some things are beyond her ability to comprehend and understand."

"Rob, I know that illustration is somewhat diminishing for you as a person with a higher intellect. In reality, the chasm that exists between God and humankind is even greater than the illustration between you and your dog Ginger."

"It is impossible for Me to explain Our Deity in terms that would clearly provide a comprehensive understanding of Our relationship to humankind, and to the universe, we created. By providing the Holy Spirit living within you, we were able to give you a sense of Our sovereignty when the Holy Spirit revealed Himself supernaturally in your life."

Jesus smiled and said, "Because We are Spirit, We can only be understood spiritually. Any understanding of Us is perceived from your spirit. The inner part of your soul was created by Us as a spirit which allows the Holy Spirit the ability to reveal and communicate truth, Spirit to spirit.

"Rob, let me give you a better understanding of Our personhood," Jesus explained.

"I am the Son the visible personification of God, if I didn't humble Myself and become a man, you would be unable to see God. No man is able to look upon God and live. It is only because I have redeemed humankind and interceded for you that you are able to look upon God through Me, at Our throne. We are Holy, and therefore no one is able to approach God unless they too are Holy. It's the imputed righteousness that my suffering and death on the cross paid, that atoned for your sin and made you righteous. My existence revolves around God's perfect expression; that is, in the creation of all things, the physical incarnation of God in man and as the intercessor of all mankind."

"Rob, I came to earth to redeem what I originally made for My good pleasure and glory. Man was created to glorify Us. We placed in your spirit the natural desire to be in a relationship with Us is written, on every man's heart. The desire to worship and obey Us. Because We gave man free will, the choice between obedience, and disobedience was necessary for Us to freely receive worship from each individual's heart. This allows each person to choose whether they will make Us Lord or make themselves their own lord. Choosing to obey Us, gives Us the glory We deserve. Man's choice in disobeying what God ordained and intended separates man from a Holy God."

"The Holy Spirit is the person of God who indwells mankind and is the spiritual power that holds everything together in the cosmos, gives life, and is the force that creates all that is good."

"The Father is the basis for all that is, will be, and has been. All Our authority comes from Him. The Father directs and orchestrates all that I do and Am, and I direct and orchestrate all that the Holy Spirit does."

"We are all equal but with different functions. As you spend more time with Me, you will come to understand the distinctness of each Person and see that We are in fact,

One. There are no human analogies that adequately describe Us. We are incomprehensible and beyond your ability to fully understand. To do so, would make you equal to Us, and that would not be possible."

"Rob imagine if men were to be gods. Think about the chaos that would occur having each god doing as they pleased. They could not coexist in harmony. In fact, that is exactly why Satan fell and no longer is the highest ranking angel. He desired to be worshipped in the same way We are worshipped, and his arrogance blinded him. There is only one God, and even the three persons that exist within the Godhead, have a hierarchal structure to coexist and be perfectly One."

Rob sat back and said, "Wow, that was enlightening. I've never quite understood the Trinity, and even now I am trying to get my mind around it. This really helps me understand who You are, and why You have made the mystery of the three persons of God, a subject that theologians have struggled with from the beginning of time."

"Rob," Jesus replied, "I know you far more than you could ever imagine, and I will reveal marvels and mysteries in increasing amounts as you are able to absorb them. Your limited knowledge base has been impeded because of your fleshly existence. Your spiritual ability to understand and retain knowledge will grow far beyond what you could ever imagine."

"You mean I can take in more information than I could on earth?" Rob asked.

"It's more than that Rob," Jesus replied.

"Yes you will be able to remember everything but more so, your capacity for what is spiritual was blocked by your fleshly body. The information was gathered in the brain, but the access and understanding was not. Now that you are in your spiritual form, there are no limits to your understanding or access. This knowledge can only be received spiritually. That's why Christians on earth are better able to understand the things God reveals to them through the Holy Spirit. Someone who does not have the Holy Spirit is unable to understand or comprehend these truths. The more a person allows the Holy Spirit to work in and through him, the more they receive understanding. It's not just about the knowledge; it's also the application and wisdom gained through the Holy Eyes of God."

CREATION

The information explained by Jesus left Rob overwhelmed. He knew that spending time before the Father would allow his spirit to connect and rest in God's infinite love. He looked at Jesus and said, "I need to worship the Father for all that I have learned."

As he said it, he was instantly before the Father's throne. The music and singing was so freeing. As the Lord's love flowed into Rob he felt at total peace with himself and the universe. The experience made him realize that as he spent more time with Jesus and the Father, the more he felt like an extension of them. Their time together was so personal and intimate that Rob stopped singing and just listened as the multitudes gave Him the glory He deserves.

Rob was worshiping before the throne of God spiritually. He realized that the expression of worship he was giving was from deep within his spirit and did not require sound. He observed other worshipers praising God in the same way. Their connection was straight from their hearts, as it was with his. Multitudes were coming and going before the throne as time passed. Many hours of blissful worship passed as the Lord's Glory permeated him completely.

He felt as though he could spend forever there before the Lord's throne of glory, but something stirred in his spirit that drew him away from his worship. The desire to know more compelled him to the Living Word.

Suddenly, he found himself in his mansion. Before him, on the table, was the Living Word. Rob still had many questions regarding the truths that are revealed in the Living Word, and he suddenly found himself opening the large beautiful book.

He decided to start at the beginning of the book. The moment he opened the book, an index appeared and below the index, a question mark. Rob thought it must be a point of reference within the book. He thought the word "creation," to himself and as he thought it, the creation of the universe began to play before him. His selection from within the Living Word knew exactly what the specific point of interest he sought, as it began to play before him.

Rob's creation journey began with him in total darkness, void of anything. Rob thought it was strange and quite a contrast compared to the incredible sights he was experiencing in heaven. Rob felt like he was there for a long period of time and he felt so alone. Time seemed to linger even though only a few of minutes had passed. Then Rob saw the Lord in all His glorious power, filling the space with brilliant light. God spoke in an inaudible language that was not understandable in human terms, mathematical in nature. It was as if word equations became matter before his eyes.

The matter at first was formless and seemed gaseous in nature. As Rob looked, he could actually see molecules form and move about in a random unformed space. It was as if he were inside an enormous microscope seeing the formation of atoms with their electrons, protons and microns, and how they were first made and then reproduced in various forms. The inner world that mankind is unable to see was magnificent and spectacular, leaving Rob feeling small and insignificant.

Then the molecules started intertwining as the intense light from God erupted in an explosive array of patterns and fractal structures. The variety was endless and infinite. Rob could see that every molecule was being held together by the power of God. He watched him create and control each molecule individually.

Rob was beginning to understand how God could know and count the hairs on every person's head. It was an enlightenment that had never occurred to him before.

The gaseous matter now began to come together as he was pulled out of the microscopic realm and into a state that was more like looking through a telescope. The black void was now filled with what appeared to be lightning bolts, emitting incredible energy and power. The power was so great it vibrated and shook the cosmos.

Then he saw the earth forming from the gaseous matter making a globe as it rotated around. As it was formed, the Lord's light penetrated the surface and its core. The surface was covered with water, and there was no visible land. Even in the raw form the earth was beautiful as the water sparkled from the light of the Lord.

There was light and darkness as the earth turned on its axis. Then the water surface erupted as energy from the Lord reined down upon the surface. The earth shook and vibrated as water was moved to some parts of the earth, separating the land from the seas. Land emerged from matter and from under the water. Massive land areas were formed.

As Rob looked upon the spectacle, he suddenly found himself hovering just above the surface and moving across the land as mountains, gorges, rock formations, and flatlands were created by the power of God. The variety seemed endless as he circled the earth at various places, observing His creative power on display.

Then, above the surface, a layer of air emerged and covered the entire planet as it rose creating a giant pocket over the surface. As the pocket increased, some of the moisture from the oceans were taken up, creating clouds of vaporized moisture. The air was pure oxygen and made Rob think of the fresh morning air after an evening snowfall, it was so refreshing and pure. The clouds formed perfect billows of soft plumes and were close to the surface, applying a cool water coating to most of the surface. The moisture set the stage for the creation of lush vegetation.

As the surface cascaded in various elevations, plants began to blossom out of the land and fill the earth. As Rob watched the plants and vegetation spread across the surface and grow from the light coming from the Lord, he could see that each plant was specifically created for the elevation and climate for the area. The Lord's light made it all spring up instantly. God's light created life and in it everything grew to perfection.

The waters were spectacular, as the erupting land structures divided large bodies of water into oceans, while others into smaller pools or lakes. The variety of the waters were as numerable as the lands. Rob could see that God's creation gave the appearance as if it were done over millions of years, even though the Lord created it in all its splendor in an instant. The thought of time being a dimension became a reality as he observed the incredible process. It was like the entire creative powers of an incomprehensible intelligence were making things as quickly as they were thought. He couldn't imagine that it was all that simple to God. He knew His power and scope were unsearchable and infinite, but to see it, was incomprehensible.

The earth looked like a huge garden with a lushness he had

only seen in heaven. The entire earth was perfect. Rob was taken into the close examination of various flora and plant life that accentuated its internal and external beauty. How wonderful it was to experience creation displayed in every form. Each flower and seed was examined and found magnificent in its own way. There were many varieties that Rob had never seen during his life on earth. The experience was powerful and life-changing, as he observed it all in wonderment.

Then just as the plants were created, Rob saw the Lord creating the sun and planets. As he saw the universe emerge, he could see that every planets distance and rotation was precisely placed. The sun was enormous and as God condensed gases together in an inferno of fire, it made the earth appear small in comparison.

Rob had never studied astronomy and didn't realize that the sun was one million times the size of earth. He also never realized the power and energy that was emitted on its surface. As the creation unfolded before him, a supernatural understanding of the scientific nature of the sun and its surrounding planets were revealed to him. The experience left him numb and feeling small in comparison to the power and glory displayed by the Lord.

Rob watched other constellations and galaxies appear, too numerable to count. Each one was created beautifully and uniquely. As he traveled to distant galaxies and constellations to experience the wonder of God's creation, the speed at which he traveled increased exponentially until it was obvious that the cosmos had no end, just as God has no beginning. The concept of infinity at first was foreign to his limited thinking that had constrained him back on earth. But as he received the sights, and experienced the unlimited power being displayed, a better understanding penetrated his mind. Rob felt like knowledge and wisdom were being poured into him.

Rob's viewing of God's creation answered so many of his questions about God and his infinite power and creativity. It also made Rob wonder about so many other things that he wanted to know. The experience was as if he were actually there. It wasn't just visual; it invoked his emotions as it played all around him like he was part of it. Obviously, it was yet another dimension created by God for seeing things in a whole new way.

The amazing variety and scope of His creation reached far beyond the understanding of human knowledge. The experience made him wonder if he were to think about a more specific question that he had, would the specifics also reveal the exact knowledge sought.

Then Rob found himself below the surface of the water. As varieties of fish appeared in a rich array of shapes and colors, he couldn't believe how the water and light enhanced the colors. The experience reminded him of the 3D movie he had seen on the oceans. But as fabulous as that was, this was as if a fourth dimension was introduced as he felt a part of the environment.

On the surface, various corals and plankton sprang up, making the contrast vibrant and yet soothing. The kaleidoscope of color against the deep blue backdrop made everything feel like he was part of creation. The Lord allowed Rob to spend a long time observing the countless creatures made specifically for their environment. He felt as if he could spend an eternity there as he moved in and out of terrain as variant as that on the surface of the earth.

As Rob exited the waters and flew across the sky, magnificent birds appeared and flew with him. God took him to every part of the world where he witnessed thousands of flying species. The thrill of flying like a bird was exhilarating. The only sounds were that of the birds singing as they were created. Rob knew that God wanted him to have the experience of what flying would be like. As he soared across the beautiful terrain and occasionally landed next to a new feathered creature to observe its uniqueness, he realized that most of human kind has no idea of the special gifts given to each creature. It is the uniqueness of every living thing that makes an infinite God beyond man's comprehension. Rob again wondered if there were any limits to the creativity of God.

Rob then flew through the sky close to the surfaces, where reptiles and dinosaurs, mighty and powerful, were roaming the lands. As other creatures were created, the expanse of time seemed to elapse leaving many of the species extinct.

Cataclysmic eruptions and weather changes altered the environment for the procreation of some animals and the elimination of others. It explained the discoveries of the dinosaurs and the earth's progression over time. As he observed the wonders of ages gone by in rapid motion, he could see other animals forming as God created every living animal one by one.

Rob was supernaturally enlightened with the knowledge of each animal, how they were created, and their uniqueness. The earth seemed to be in perfect harmony as the orchestration of life was observed and the expansion of life unfolded before him.

Rob saw other insects and microscopic life forms appear as they were created in even a greater number and variety than all other creatures combined. Seeing the life forms within and at their habitation revealed a wonderful world Rob never knew existed. Even that was perfectly produced to provide balance and harmony in each eco system.

Rob wondered how anyone could ever think that this could have happened without a creator. If only those who believed in evolution could see what he was seeing, they would be ashamed at their stupidity and foolishness.

The pinnacle of the experience was when God took Rob to a beautiful garden. There where rivers that cascaded about and lush trees, filled with fruits, lined their shores. The flora and vegetation were much like those in heaven.

As he stood there in awe, suddenly, from the ground, came a swirling light that illuminated the matter upon the earth. From the light a form materialized. He could see that it was a very complex creation with an inner soul that God had placed uniquely inside its body. The shape eventually formed into what Rob would describe as a perfect man. His beauty and structure looked meticulously carved and magnificent. At first the form appeared dead, but then a visible Spirit came down from above, breathing life into the body.

Then Rob was taken inside the microscopic world that no person has ever seen. He watched the inner molecular structures form the DNA chains that uniquely form humans. The intricacy and intellectual composition of God's limitless creativity was displayed. It took Rob's breath away as he became enlightened about the human makeup. Then Rob toured the various organs and bio-machineries that are intricate and beyond human understanding. Seeing these marvelous wonders in their intricate order made the time pass before him in a flash.

Then Rob watched as God came and spoke with the man and said, "I have made this land for you and you are made in My image. This land is for you to rule. You will name all the birds of the air, beasts of the fields and all living creatures."

Then God said, "It is not good for you to be alone, so I will make you a suitable helper."

While the man slept, God took one of his ribs and from it, created a woman.

When he awoke and saw her, he said, "I will call her woman

because she is bone of my bones and flesh of my flesh."

Then God told them that they were to populate the earth and rule over it. God saw that it was very good and as they were united as husband and wife, they became one in spirit. They were both naked but because there was no sin, they felt no shame.

As Rob finished observing the beginning of mankind, he thought about Kate. He wondered how she was and what she would be doing. The wonder of all the activities had made Rob forget about those he left back on earth. It hit him, that as great as it was being in heaven, it would be so much better if his loved ones were all present to experience this with him. He knew that eventually, they would be there with him. The void was still there, and he would have to wait until their time on earth was completed.

Universe

Jesus appeared as Rob sat thinking about his family back on earth. The memories flooded Rob's mind as he reflected on how much he loved them.

"I thought that you could use some recreation and fun to get your mind off of your family," said Jesus.

Rob asked, "So, what do have in mind?"

Jesus smiled and said, "We can go anywhere you would like, and do whatever you can imagine."

Rob looked puzzled. "What do you mean?" he asked.

"Well, I'll take you anywhere in the universe. If you would like, we can visit another galaxy, or explore a planet, or enjoy speeding through space. What's your desire?" Jesus asked.

Rob loved the feeling of traveling fast, and remembered a ride he went on at Disney World that made him feel as if he were traveling through space and time.

Rob smiled, and said, "You know me better than I know myself, so you pick the trip, but make it thrilling and fast."

Suddenly Rob and Jesus were catapulted through space accelerating steadily until they were moving faster than the speed of light. The speed made Rob hyperventilate. Rob couldn't believe he was moving like this, as if he were super human. He looked down at himself, as his soul body was flying next to Jesus through outer space and laughed with delight as their speed continued to increase.

They raced by planets and solar systems. They rapidly changed directions as Jesus traversed the heavens, avoiding collisions with various objects. Jesus seemed to delight in knowing the thrill Rob was feeling and laughed with him, as pleasure and joy filled Rob completely.

They slowed from time to time, so Rob could see the infinite variety of planetary formations with their unique beauty. Rob was in wonder of the scope of God's Creation and the power that was displayed before him. Rob was unable to speak because the experience was so overwhelming. His soul cried out within him, that God was so much more than he could have ever imagined.

"Rob, all physical matter was created for you and for those who have chosen Me as their Lord. I love showing these physical manifestations of our creativity so mankind can better understand who We Are," Jesus said.

Jesus suddenly stopped their travel. They were now floating in space and Jesus revealed to Rob that everything was being held together by Him, down to the smallest components within atoms. Rob wanted to fall down before Him in worship as he realized how insignificant he was as compared to Him.

Jesus turned and looked into Rob's eyes and said, "Rob, please understand that you are significant. You are what We designed you to be. We created you for ourselves. You have recognized and glorified Us and that is what We sought when you were created. You want to fall down before Me because of who I am. That gives Me glory, and I love being glorified freely."

Rob suddenly understood that without him freely submitting to God's authority and Lordship, his worship would be meaningless to God. He realized that God could have demanded that all mankind worship and bow before Him, but giving each person a choice, makes it true worship and true glorification. This was the first time Rob fully understood how Jesus could find such enjoyment in relationships with His creation.

As they continued to travel through space, very solar system was different and the variety was so incredible that Rob wondered if there was any limitation to God's power and creativity.

Jesus answered his question by saying, "We are all powerful and our abilities have no limits. I know that's a difficult concept for you but we will continue to display Our Power, Our love, and Our mysteries for all to see. It gives Us pleasure to see our creation marvel at Our attributes that show who We are."

There were a variety of planets with differing characteristics and elements.

Jesus said, "We made the matter different and unique in each system. That's what makes their appearance and majesty endless in beauty and splendor. Our creativity declares Our glory to all who see it. Rob, you will experience these sights with Me forever."

Jesus took Rob into a black hole where Rob could feel God's incredible power. The experience was exhilarating as Jesus held them stationary, as space and matter were pulled into a limitless mass.

"Rob," Jesus explained, "We created the black hole to show that through Us, all things are possible even though there is no rational explanation. We chose to confound the intelligence of the brightest minds ever known to display how unknowable We are. The more science reveals the more confounding it becomes to those who study it. Scientists must eventually conclude that We created it and that

We are far beyond, anyone's knowledge."

They suddenly shot down toward a planet where the atmosphere appeared in oscillating colors both vibrant and pure. Jesus showed him life forms that were totally different than those on earth and in heaven. Jesus took him along the landscape and over surfaces that reflected back the vibrant colors that illuminated the sky.

Jesus said, "How do you like this place Rob?"

Rob wanted to stay there and learn more about it, because it was so different from anything he had ever seen before.

"Rob," Jesus said, "There are planets throughout the universe that can be explored and experienced, each unique and special. They are innumerable and you will be able to enjoy them forever. That is why, when We created them, We declared that, it is good."

Rob asked if there was intelligent life on these other planets.

Jesus said, "Yes, but not like humankind. You were made unique because you were made in Our image, and there are no other creatures that were created to have the intimate relationship that you are enjoying with Us. We created humankind as creative beings that are fulfilled by using their unique giftedness to give Us glory and to show love to others."

Jesus took Rob down to examine some of the life forms on the planet. Rob found it fascinating, as he observed several beautiful creatures eating from a fruit tree. He thought how strange they appeared. Then one of them communicated with another in a strange language that had a musical tone and a pleasing rhythm.

Rob looked at Jesus and asked, "Is it possible to understand what they are saying?"

"Sure Rob," Jesus replied, and then as the creatures spoke to one another, Rob could understand what they were saying. They were discussing their need to gather food for others who were hungry. Rob was surprised by their demeanor that seemed so harmonious and friendly.

Jesus smiled and said, "We created them with a pure heart; there is no sin here. They have no choice to choose evil, because it doesn't exist here. Therefore, they love completely and only act in accordance to the nature that we have given them."

Rob seemed surprised by the explanation, and asked; "Will humankind ever live like that, without sin?"

"Yes, Rob," Jesus replied, "all Our children will live harmoniously on the new earth that is to come. Evil will be taken out of the world leaving behind the selfishness that deceives the current world."

How joyful these creatures were as they gathered food for others. Rob thought as Jesus took him into a large canyon that sparkled like a jewel. There the creatures were gathered together for fellowship as they ate. They shared their provisions freely with one another as they enjoyed their love for one another that was obvious among them.

Jesus smiled and said, "These are some of my favorite creations because they live in simplicity and unity. Their unselfish love for one another makes a perfect society. Because sin has not entered this place, there is no need to discipline them or control them. They live eternally because there is no disease. They are physical beings that regenerate themselves as they sleep. Each of them knows exactly what their role is in this utopian society. There is a hierarchy within this creation that provides a specific purpose and fulfillment to each one individually, and then, together, as a group. This canyon is their home because it provides everything they need."

"We only created one male and one female, as we did with Adam and Eve. They enjoy the process of mentoring and uniting intimately through their unselfish nature that lives in harmony as an ever growing family. They can only have one child every twenty years which allows each child to be raised and mentored individually."

Rob wondered why Jesus didn't create mankind that way.

Jesus knowing his thoughts said, "Rob, Adam and Eve were created with a spirit that had many of the attributes We possess. Those attributes were given so that Mankind could have a relationship with Us. That special and personal relationship had to include the option of choice. That choice was in deciding lordship."

"When Satan fell, We decided to send him to the earth where Adam and Eve could choose to obey Us, or the lies that We knew Satan would impose on them. We knew it would be the price that was necessary to test the free will of mankind. Allowing Satan access to mankind was also a way for Us to confine his power, and domain, rather than allowing him to ravage the universe as a whole."

"As a result of Satan's pride, he thought that by deceiving humankind, he too would be a god and be glorified by Adam and Eve."

"Satan knew that God could not have a relationship with man once he sinned because of His holiness. His plan was to make the earth his domain like the Father has made heaven. Before sin entered the world, We walked with Our creation, and they had a wonderful relationship with Us. When man decided to disobey the Father's command, that relationship ended. Satan and his followers were banned from the Garden, along with Adam and Eve, as a result of both their disobedient acts."

"Because the Father loves mankind, He allowed Me to become a man and live among humankind. I was tempted in all things, just as man is tempted, but I did not sin. I humbled Myself allowing my suffering, shame, and then death on the cross, to atone for sin once and for all. When I rose from the grave, Satan and his plan were defeated. Mankind now has the ultimate choice to choose My free gift of atonement, that allows a relationship with Us again."

"Rob, before you were formed, I knew you. I knew all that you would do, all that you would desire, and all that you loved to do. Every hair on your head was counted, every breath recorded, every cell in your body was purposely chosen. I gave you your unique DNA and gifted you for a greater purpose. I kept you close through my word, and protected you from evil.

Are you surprised that the fate of each person is known? You are one of the Father's children who he dearly loves. It is My desire to do the Father's will which provides for eternal joy and fulfillment to be available to everyone. But even though I know before the foundation of time each decision, it remains every person's choice. That is the mystery of man's choice versus Our election in salvation. That process involves Our drawing to a relationship that can only be found in Us and the yielding to that drawing that We place in everyone's heart."

Rob finally understood the mystery of God's election, but was still overwhelmed by the experience. He was wondering about how he could grasp all that he was experiencing as they explored the universe together.

He finally asked, "How does all this exist at your will? The scope and breath of what I've seen is just so overwhelming. It's hard for me to grasp Your mysteries."

Jesus explained, "We hold every molecule together by Our will. All life in any form is from Us. Without Us, life could not exist. Our power and capacity is limitless, Our attributes indescribable, and Our knowledge boundless. We know all, see all, and are all that is. Remember Rob, My description given in Scripture of Myself is: I Am. We created the earth and all living things along with the universe in seven days in all of its splendor. So then, creating the universe specifically for you is, for Us, a small thing. You had limited access to Me until now, and because of your limited access, it made these concepts difficult to fully comprehend. That will change as your knowledge and understanding of Us increases."

"Rob," Jesus explained, "Your ability to retain knowledge is limitless. You will retain everything you see, read, and experience. Remember how you always wished you had a photographic memory while you were in college? Well now you do! Your wisdom will grow more each day as you absorb the knowledge and experiences I have prepared for you. Rob, I will continue to amaze and delight you. You will also experience the special things that those who are co-heirs with you delight in."

"When you were on earth, all that you saw, learned, and experienced, was recorded in your soul, even though you couldn't recall all of it because of your flesh. The limitations of your flesh prevented total access of that information. Here you do not have the flesh interfering with that access. That is why when you arrived in Heaven and I met with you, and then touch you, I exposed every sin, every deed, good or bad to you. For the first time you were able to access that information. I prompted you, through the Holy Spirit, to access all of that stored information that was stored in your memory. They were all written there. Then I destroyed any sin reigning in your soul, so you are now pure and blameless because the penalty for that sin was paid through Me. The information is still there but the atonement through Me removed the penalty. Here you will be able to recall everything."

"That is why the souls that have been sent to Hades (hell) become increasingly evil. If all that they see, learn, and experience, is rooted in sin and evil, then the manifestation of that information is additional evil. Love for their Maker is replaced by hatred."

"Here all things are pure and you have been made pure. Your increasing knowledge and your experiences will draw you ever closer to your creator God. You are becoming wise and have knowledge, rightly applied living within you now. As you grow in knowledge and wisdom, you can do greater things, understand deeper meanings, and glorify the Father in an ever increasing way by living under His will. That is why the angels, who have proven themselves faithful, seek to do the Father's will. It is the pinnacle of their joy."

"There is no disintegration of any kind here because all regeneration is from Us. All things are as they were when We created them; they are continually new, nothing wears out, and everything is indestructible. What was precious and rare on earth We now made plentiful and common here. The very things humankind held in the highest esteem, we have made into the foundation of the city. That's why the streets are made of pure gold and the foundation and walls of precious stones, and best of all, the light comes from the Father. All things here are perfect and new, and they will never pass away or diminish."

Rob felt like he needed to spend more time before the Father's throne. His inner being kept calling him to return to the great throne-room and worship the Father. He thought about asking Jesus to excuse himself, because he really felt led to go before the Father. His desire to worship there was always present but somehow he knew that it was where he belonged at that moment. Each time he went there, the glory that came from God was so incredible that it left him filled with energy and excitement. It was definitely the best experience that there is, better than everything else combined.

Two Ways to an End

When he decided that he wanted to go before the throne, he was instantly there. Seeing the universe in all its glory required a response. Rob's spirit was overflowing. He was surprised when he saw Jesus next to the Father because he had just left Him.

Jesus moved toward Rob and said, "I am omnipresent and can be present in as many places as I choose to, at once. Rob intellectually knew this, but to actually experience it was something else."

Rob felt foolish for thinking Jesus was just spending time with him.

There were angels singing and praising the Lord as far as he could see. Rob had to catch his breath as the sight of God's glory and radiance made him surge with energy and excitement. The music was beautiful and instantly drew him into worship. There was an intimacy that Rob was experiencing that only pure love from the Father could extend, and Rob was soaring in his spirit as he worshiped and fell before Him in gratitude.

There was something about the collective worship, when angels and God's elect gather before Him. The number of people and angels present were like the sands of the seashore, beyond counting. The sound was so powerful it made Rob tremble at God's glory. As he watched messengers come and go before the Lord to receive their instructions, he knew that although he didn't know it, when he lived on earth, he was made for this purpose; to bow and to worship the Creator of the universe forever.

Rapture

Jesus knew Rob was thinking about the separation he felt from his wife and family. The experience of worshiping before the Father's throne and the experience of witnessing God's infinite creation made him want Kate there all the more. Jesus came over to Rob as he thought about them. Rob seemed surprised when he looked up and saw Jesus standing there with his hand held out to help Rob up from his knees as he worshipped God. Instantly he found himself sitting in his mansion with Jesus smiling at him as He sat across from him. Jesus asked if he liked the experiences from their journey through creation and the universe.

Rob looked at Him and said, "It was beyond what any words could describe, and it has changed my view of everything."

Rob was thinking about Kate and how she, being the scientific type, would love seeing this. Rob paused, and then asked Jesus, "At creation, you made a helper for man, and they became one flesh. Why is it that no one here is in a marriage relationship?"

"Good question Rob," Jesus replied, "but let me ask you a question first. Have you ever felt lonely here? Have you ever felt like you needed someone to help you with anything here?"

Two Ways to an End

Rob thought for a moment and replied, "Well no, not really."

Jesus then said, "Why do you think that is Rob?"

"Well, I suppose it's because we are not needy here."

Jesus had a subtle smile that expressed something more meaningful was about to be explained.

"Rob," Jesus said, "It's a bit more complicated than that. Remember when I told you that here the source of everything comes from the Father?"

Rob shook his head and answered, "Sure, I remember."

"Well, that source replaces the need that you have to complete you, just as the woman did before. We gave woman to man primarily for intimacy and relationship, because he was alone. Here, procreation is not necessary because you and everyone here will live forever therefore, a spouse is not necessary. You will have deep and intimate relationships with everyone here, and of course, you have Me, the Father, and the Holy Spirit to love and guide you."

"Here in heaven, you are complete and need nothing because everything comes from Us: the Father, Myself, and the Holy Spirit. The only thing you are experiencing that makes you feel a void, is the fact that you want those who you love, to feel what you are feeling. That's because you love them. When you think about them being here with you, it isn't because you need them here, it's because you want them to feel like you feel. It's like the feeling you have when you give someone a gift that you know they will love. You do it because you know it will give them joy, and giving them joy, gives you joy."

Rob processed what Jesus was saying and asked, "So when will I see them?"

Jesus knew the question was coming and said, "The time is now short for my return. Kate will be here prior to that time, but your daughter and grandchildren will experience my triumphal return."

Rob seemed curious about the timing, and then Jesus said, "No man knows the hour of my return. Only the Father knows when that will occur. Rob, if you knew the exact time, you would want to spend time focusing on it, and as much as you want them here, they are needed on earth to carry out the Father's will. You will be united with them soon enough."

Rob had always wondered about when the rapture was to occur and how it would happen. So he asked Jesus, "What exactly happens at the rapture?"

"Rob," Jesus replied, "when I return, the Church will be taken up into the air, and they will all be with me. All believers will in one moment be looking up because they will hear the trumpet sound, and My command as the Archangel announces My entry. They will see Me coming down from heaven. First, the believers that were martyred for my sake will be resurrected. Then those whose bodies are in the grave will be raised with Me in heaven. They will ascend to heaven as their bodies are resurrected from the grave, and joined with their souls, then transfigured. Every believer will be given their new glorified bodies that are imperishable. From the graves, bodies will arise and meet their souls in the air as they are transformed, transfigured, and glorified."

"Then in a moment, all the saints living on earth that have made Me Lord and accepted My free gift of salvation, will be removed from the earth and will be caught up with Me in the clouds."

"The resurrected bodies and the bodies of those who were brought up while living, are then changed in an instant. Their bodies will look like Mine and their abilities will be far greater than anything seen before, on earth and in heaven."

As Rob looked at Jesus, His body glistened with an inner brilliance.

Then Jesus said, "When you see them, they will experience the joy of being My bride as they are transformed. As the myriads of believers are taken up into the air, the Glory will radiate from My presence drawing them all before Me. I will meet each one as they come and welcome them. As their iniquities are removed from their hearts, they will stand blameless before the Father. Eventually they will approach the heavenly throne where there will be singing and worshipping like never before, as the celebration of all the angels and risen souls of the children of God, sing songs of praise and worship. Every person will be overwhelmed by the experience, and as their gratitude grows before the Father, they will fall down and praise Him. An infinite number of angels will be everywhere, and their joyful praise will fill Heaven with sounds so glorious no one will be able to stand."

"Every person whose name is written in the Lamb's Book of Life will be judged and rewarded for their life that was lived on earth. Each person's sinful acts will be removed leaving only their righteous acts to be displayed before the Father. Each person will receive rewards for their righteous acts. They will receive rewards beyond anything that can be imagined. These rewards will be eternal and will forever be enjoyed by everyone whos name is written in the Lamb's Book of Life and have made Jesus their Lord."

"Upon receiving their rewards, they will lay them before the Father in gratitude and reverence. The Father's desire is that each reward would be received and enjoyed. This is His expression of His love for all who have lived righteously. Crowns will be given as their rewards are acknowledged and rewarded. Many will be kings and queens in this new realm where everyone will reign with Me forever."

Rob knew the event would be wonderful but as Jesus described it, the anticipation grew inside him, desiring that the day would come soon. Rob wanted his family to experience the joy of this place and the intimacy that he felt.

Jesus looked at Rob, and said, "The day of my return will usher in joy for all who believe, but also a time of suffering for those who are left behind. The Father's wrath that has been held back for the sake of the saints will be released, and the unsaved will endure many painful things. His wrath will bring an end to the corruption that fills the earth and its inhabitants."

"When the Church is raised and goodness is removed from the earth, mankind will turn to total darkness and curse the name of God. Their evil will bring God's wrath upon them and their days will be numbered. When the great deceiver, who is the devil, rules the world and then martyrs the elect, the Father will withdraw His Spirit. Most of those left behind will harden their hearts and reject the free gift of salvation. Many will be deceived by the rise of the antichrist and the powers of darkness. He will come disguised as a peacemaker, but his ways are destructive and evil. Most living in those final days will follow him and receive his mark. It is with sadness that mankind will turn away from me and follow the false prophet, the dragon, and the beast. They will bring destruction to the world and to those who follow them. Satan will know that his time is short, and will seek to remove as many souls from my redemption as he can."

"Satan and his followers will be cast out of heaven forever. The spiritual war that takes place in the heavenlies will leave Satan and his followers full of fury. He will focus on destroying and deceiving all living souls on earth. As he inflicts his evil on the earth, and destroys it, I will return and have him cast into the lake of fire for 1,000 years."

"Until that time, the earth will experience hardship and evil like never before. He will desecrate My Holy Temple in Jerusalem, and declare himself god. He will set up his kingdom to mimic Our sovereignty and convince many people of the world that he is god. He and his false prophets will make all humankind bow to him, or they will die. The remaining saints who accept salvation will be martyred and given a special place in the kingdom."

Rob wanted to know how anyone who was left on earth after the rapture would be able to turn to the Lord, if there was no one there to explain salvation.

Jesus answered, "Many that heard the message before the rapture will remember that believers would be taken up. When this actually happens, many will repent and believe. Their grief from the taking of their loved ones who believed will motivate them to believe as well. Then they will take up their cross and become witnesses to salvation through Me. The Father will also send Moses and Elijah to Jerusalem to proclaim the truth and to prophesize of the wrath that is to come. They will warn all the people of the earth to repent. Many Jews will come to faith as a result of their witness. The Devil will try to destroy them, but for a season they will be protected, and nothing will harm them. Many people will not turn to God, and then will hate them for their testimony."

"The final wrath of God will be poured out upon humanity and the last three and one half years and will consume most everyone in the world. They will suffer at the Fathers hand forever. As a last attempt to reach those who would receive My gift, a series of events will unfold that point to the redemption and sovereignty of the Father. We seek to allow every living person an opportunity to believe and receive Me, as their Savior. Only a select few will turn and repent of their sin and ask for salvation. We are grieved at the hardness of the human heart. The war between the truth that is evident throughout the earth and the deceptions of the devil reigning in the heart of each individual."

"As for those who do accept My salvation, they will be held in special honor because they will have endured incredible suffering, and death, at the hand of Satan. Their reward will triumph at the throne as they are rewarded and crowned by the Father. The first half of the seven year tribulation will be mild compared to the final wrath that is poured out at the end."

Rob was glad that Jesus was explaining the events rather than actually seeing them unfold. He didn't think that he could endure seeing so many people suffer at the hand of Satan. Rob knew that the wrath of God would be just. The thought and reality of those who would have unsaved loved ones left behind, gripped him. He thought about opportunities lost when he was on earth that might have redeemed a person from eternal judgment and condemnation.

Jesus saw that Rob was struggling with his failure in reaching more people, and said, "Everyone that comes here regrets that they were not bolder when they lived on earth. The unveiling of truth and love motivates everyone. Remember Rob, no one has a good excuse to reject Me on earth. I revealed Myself to all and My creation screams out that I exist. It is the darkness of their own hearts that condemns them. Your life on earth was a witness to others just by the way that you lived. Don't underestimate the seeds that you planted, there were many."

Rob pondered the assurance that Jesus expressed, and replied, "I know that we only have a short time on earth to make an impact. If only those who believe knew how vital it is to reach the lost, they would have different priorities. I know that I would have. As I think about where I spent most of my time and effort, I regret the missed opportunities."

As he looked into Rob's eyes with compassion, Jesus replied. "Your life on earth was a joy to Me and to the angels who watched over you. You discovered the true meaning of life, a relationship with Me."

Rob blushed and said, "You give me too much credit. I was very selfish in many ways. You know that I was far from perfect."

Jesus smiled and said, "That may be true, but you always repented and came back to what was important. Don't underestimate your impact through your service to Me, and others around you. It was a life lived, for the most part, in loving God and loving people. That was a life well lived Rob. Your sinful nature made you imperfect and that's why I came. It was to complete you and allow you to reflect My goodness and love to others through you. None are without sin and there is no way to earn your way to salvation, it is my free gift to all who will receive it."

Time with Mom

Rob needed a break from all that he had experienced and absorbed and longed for some loving fellowship. The explanation of the rapture and the remaining events that would occur left him drained and distraught.

When Jesus looked at him, a supernatural comfort entered him.

Jesus said, "I know the perfect thing for you right now."

Then in an instant, Rob found himself in front of a large door made of jasper. The door and entrance sparkled and reflected light over him as he stood there in awe. He wondered where he was, then the door opened and his mom stood there with open arms.

"Jesus told me you were coming," she said. "I have so much to share with you. Come in Rob, and welcome to my home."

Rob was so happy to see his mom, she was always there to comfort him when he needed her love.

As he hugged her he said, "I love you Mom, and I'm so glad that I am here with you."

She smiled and said, "Your dad and I have longed for the day when you and the family would join us. We knew that because of your faith and the love of our Lord, you would one day join us here in Heaven."

Rob's mom could see from his demeanor that Rob was feeling badly about the final outcome of all mankind. Learning about the events after the rapture and during the tribulation was weighing on Rob's heart. She knew he was thinking about how many people would spend eternity in hell.

"Rob" she said, "Knowing the outcome of mankind is one of the realities we must accept. I was so sad and burdened by the outcome when Jesus explained it to me. Then I realized that even God Himself would not prevent them from choosing evil over righteousness, it is each individual's decision. God could force all humankind to obey and follow Him at His will because He is omnipotent. But in doing so, mankind would merely be puppets. Imagine how much more it saddens our Lord, who loves perfectly when humans choose evil over righteousness. We can't even come close to the grief He feels over His creation."

"Those events must happen to purge the universe of evil and sin. Without free will and choice, we would be mere slaves in His presence. The reward for Him is the joy He sees in us, as we freely give of ourselves to Him. The glory we give Him that rightly deserves is the greatest gift of all. We were created for worship and adoration. When we turn from our own ways and seek Him, only then are we satisfied and fulfilled."

As Rob looked around, he could see the mansion had his mom's personality written all over it. Rob's mom loved knickknacks and things that bordered on garish. She spent much of her time while she was on earth creating colorful afghans and quilts as Rob was growing up. Spaces throughout her mansion were filled with frilly items ideal to meet her tastes.

"How do you like it Rob?" she asked excitedly.
"It's all you Mom, I love it!" Rob replied.

"Thanks Rob, let me show you around. This place is so big that I sometimes forget about some of the rooms I have here."

As she gave Rob a tour, he could tell that she loved her home and thought it was the best mansion in heaven.

Jesus had created each room to fit perfectly with the nuances of his mom's personality and tastes. She was so happy and excited, as she showed him every room and then all the personal items in the rooms that made the home so special to her. Rob could see she had many rooms, as a result of her many interests and hobbies. Rob knew she would never get bored here.

She had a special quilting room set up with all the materials and equipment needed for her hobby. There were exotic fabrics, spectacular and rich and beautiful in color and texture. Some of the laces were made in the room on a machine invented by Rob's dad. Rob was delighted that his dad was busy inventing machines here in heaven just as he had back on earth.

Rob's mom was an avid reader, she had a library with thousands of books. She explained that the books were able to be experienced as they were read, much like the Living Word. The library overlooked a garden and had a large padded lounge chair that looked very inviting.

Many of the rooms were intended for her time spent with Rob's dad. There was a small dining area that had cozy little chairs and a frilly white table cloth set with beautiful china. It was exactly what his mom loved and fit perfectly in the setting.

She smiled and said, "This is where your dad and I have dinner most nights. There is so much to talk about here that we seem to lose track of ourselves and before we know it, more than a day has passed. Our relationship was good when we were back on earth, but nothing like it is here. When Kate arrives, you will be amazed at how perfect your love for her will be. We are so very happy here."

She took Rob to a large outdoor terrace that was surrounded by lush flora and a smooth shiny floor. She stood there with a huge smile on her face and said, "I'll bet your wondering what this terrace is for?" she asked.

"I'd love to know," Rob replied.

She went over to a large digital array on the wall and pressed several buttons. Music from every direction began to play.

Rob couldn't believe his eyes as he saw his mom dancing as if she were in a Russian ballet. She was spectacular and danced effortlessly to the music. Her athleticism was remarkable and made Rob wonder why he never knew about her talent. She came over and asked him to dance with her. Rob was surprised when he started dancing to the music and moved effortlessly to the rhythm.

He laughed and said, "This is so much fun Mom."

"Rob, I dance for your father here every day."

Rob looked up and saw his dad across from them on his terrace next door smiling as he watched them.

"Sometimes I dance with your father. He has become quite the dancer himself."

Rob thought for a moment and wondered if the talents were enhanced here for everyone or, if it was just that way for some. He would have to remember to ask Jesus about this experience. It was amazing how Jesus could explain things in such a simple yet profound way. His ability to reveal truth and unveil mysteries made Rob want to know more. He felt selfish because he was having so much fun, and the experiences were so joyful. To think that each day would bring a new experience; a new lesson, a new emotion, a new memory, a new piece of information, and an increase in his understanding of God. It was beyond bliss, it was heaven.

After much dancing, singing and frolicking to the music, she stopped and said, "Let's go for a walk."

She wanted to let Rob know that there were times when he was growing up, when she wasn't the mom she thought she should have been. Rob smiled as she confessed the inadequacies that she felt from an imperfect life. She asked him if he would forgive her for her shortcomings.

He turned and looked into her eyes and smiled broadly. "Mom, you were the best! I wouldn't trade you for all the other mom's in the world."

She smiled back, hugged him and said, "I love you Rob!"

She ended the tour on the upper level. There was a crystal recliner facing a lush garden that filled the patio with wonderful aromas. Her Living Word Book was there next to the recliner on a small table.

"This is where I spend a considerable amount of time Rob. I've become quite a student of the Word. The more I study it, the more I want to be in it. It's almost as good as being with Jesus or in front of the Father. How great is this place Rob, just wait until Kate and the rest of the family join us."

Rob looked down and saw his dad waving at him from a golden balcony that had a walkway leading to another mansion.

Is that Dad?" He asked.

"Yes he lives next door and Jesus made us a walkway so we can visit each other whenever we feel like it."

"That's great Mom. I guess Jesus has thought of everything. I wondered why there seemed to be an empty space next to my mansion. It must be for Kate's mansion when she arrives."

"If that's the desire of your heart, I'm sure that will become a reality." She replied.

Rob's mom asked, "So what's next for you?"

Rob seemed preoccupied and deep in thought.

"Well Mom," he replied, "I need to get back to Jesus for some additional insights. Jesus is going to guide me through the millennium and then the judgment. The final scene will be the creation of the new heaven and new earth. I can't wait to see what it will be like."

Rob's mom understood and had experienced a similar reaction after she experienced the final judgments.

"Please come by and visit us, your dad is like a little kid in a candy store and he has something to give you," she replied.

As he sought to be in the Living Word again with Jesus, he suddenly found himself right where they had left off. Jesus was there to explain the events that were about to unfold.

Jesus said, "I want you to see something. I'm going to take you into the future to see me coming down from Heaven."

Rob suddenly saw a multitude of people gathered for war in a large valley where he saw the horrific scene of destruction and carnage of humans. The scene was replaced by Jesus coming down to earth as the angels announced his entry from heaven. His appearance was spectacular and sensational and brought a chill down Rob's spine. Jesus dazzled as the brightness of his glory, which was even brighter than He was in heaven filled the entire earth.

Those who remained on earth fell down in horror at His holy presence. Many who accepted His gift of salvation worshipped Him because they had given their lives over to Him. There were 144,000 Jews who were witnesses during the tribulation singing songs of praise as he descended. All the other tribulation saints, who were not killed and were saved during the tribulation, would now live during the millennium.

But for those who did not believe and followed Satan and his world order, it was a horrific scene of destruction and carnage of humans. Jesus cut the scene short by saying, "It would not be good for you to see the wrath that I will bring on them." The scene was replaced by the New Jerusalem coming down from heaven.

Rob could see a brightly lit city coming down upon the earth. Its beauty was something to behold as Jesus took His rightful seat on the throne in the middle of the city. His glory filled the city and then went out and healed the earth. The destruction and rubble were replaced with clear skies, lush vegetation and topography that was even more spectacular than His original creation. The animals and living creatures that were annihilated reappeared and lived in harmony with one another.

Those who were still living, and accepted Jesus as their Lord during the tribulation, did not age or have disease. They procreated and prospered as Jesus reined from Jerusalem with an iron fist. God's elect who were killed or died before or during the tribulation and were resurrected, came and went as they co-led the affairs of God with Jesus on earth.

Every Knee Will Bow

Rob was again with Jesus as he concluded his tour of the 1,000 year millennium. The tour revealed how much God desires that every person would turn to Him as their Personal Savior. Even with Him in their presence, many who were born and living under His authority during the millennium would not accept Him as their Lord. As the millennium entered its end, Satan was released along with his legions of angels for a final conflict.

"He will once again deceive the people of all nations and gather them from the four corners of the earth for battle," Jesus explained.

Jesus then took him to a scene and as Rob looked, he saw a sea of people, like the sands of the earth, gather around the Holy City where God's people live. Then Rob saw the great white throne of God and the multitudes that gathered there were those martyred in the name of Jesus.

Many, who were born on the new earth during the millennium, turned and followed Satan. Multitudes gathered rejecting the Lordship of Jesus even though His reign was among them. Their hearts were hardened as they believed the lies of Satan. Mankind is deceived, because they think that they are not subject to the Lordship of Jesus. Now they will suffer in the lake of fire forever as a result of their arrogance.

Rob couldn't help but wonder why so many could be deceived by Satan so easily. Their blind and hardened hearts were once again turned to Satan and his deceptive promises of power and prosperity. How could mankind turn from the truth as it was displayed before them in His glory. They choose to follow the lies of Satan, knowing his deception had brought an end to all those who did not believe on the earth 1,000 years earlier.

Jesus said, "Satan is the author of all lies and has no truth in him. He knows that his time is short, and will do anything to steal the souls of God's children. He hates Us, and all that are Ours. Many have deceived themselves in thinking that they are in control and their selfishness blinds them from truth. Unfortunately, they will suffer in hell as a result of their wickedness."

Rob watched God's elect and the nation of Israel gather together in the Holy City. There, God would protect them from the slaughter that was about to take place. Jesus explained that it would be better if he didn't see the horror that they would go through at the final judgment. Rob knew Jesus was right, and he decided to forgo the experience.

"Rob," Jesus said, "It's important for you to see the end of Satan and his followers. Never again will he deceive and destroy God's children. He will suffer in accordance to what he has done, and all will see him cast forever into the lake of fire. His torment will have no end. The martyred saints will finally receive their justice."

Rob watched as Michael the Archangel seized Satan and threw him into the lake of fire. There he will suffer with the beast and the false prophet, who deceived mankind before the millennium. They will be tormented by fire and burning

Two Ways to an End

sulfur, day and night forever and ever.

He was surprised by the power of the large angel. His majesty was almost as spectacular as the physical appearance of Jesus. He glowed with pure light and the energy from within his being was increasing. Rob seemed surprised at how easily he subdued Lucifer and bound him. God must have given Michael special powers to subdue Satan that easily. Satan spewed out blasphemies as a heavenly host of powerful angels escorted him to the lake of fire. As he was thrown into the lake of fire, God removed his supernatural powers.

Then, Rob saw lightning and thunder and a great earthquake shake the earth off its axis. The noise was deafening as these cataclysmic events erupted before his eyes. Cities fell and melted away. The earth's crust broke open consuming everything. The earth's atmosphere disintegrated and burned with fire as it passed away.

Those who were gathered for battle through the deceptions of the Devil, were slaughtered and their souls taken before the Great White Throne of God where each would be judged by their deeds. All the souls whose names are not in the book of life will be judged.

They will come before Jesus where every knee will bow, and every tongue confess, that Jesus Christ is Lord of all. Their transgressions will be judged according to what they had done during their life on earth. Each act is recorded in books where all their deeds are exposed. Rob watched as all those who rejected the free gift of life came before the Great White Throne of God. Each came before the Lord and the books were opened revealing every deed done throughout their life. Their most righteous deeds were vial compared to the righteousness of a Holy God. As their deeds are revealed and displayed before them, they fell to their knees and confess "Jesus is Lord."

They were each judged based upon every deed that was

done and sentenced to their eternal damnation in the lake of fire. Each individual would suffer forever for their transgressions, and for the unpardonable sin, which is the rejection of Jesus. They now knew their own depravity and became increasingly evil as they cursed God and were cast into the lake of fire forever.

Their suffering and torment will be beyond anything that can be imagined. Never ending pain and isolation will be endured by those who chose to believe Satan's lie. Their choice of rejecting Jesus was given during their one and only life in the flesh on earth. They chose not to believe, and receive God's gift of forgiveness. That choice will ultimately determine their eternal place of isolation. How foolish was their choice. How often were they presented with the truth? The reality is that every person is without excuse. Wide is the path that leads to eternal damnation, and narrow is the way that leads to eternal joy in paradise.

Rob watched Hades which holds all those captive who are not saved by the grace of God. They are thrown into the lake of fire, where Satan was sent before them. There will be wailing and gnashing of teeth because they rejected the truth. They will suffer forever. There is no relief, no escape, and no way to repent. Their choice was made on earth, and the consequence of their choice will cost them eternal damnation. The evil that deceived the people and the fallen demons will torment them forever.

It was revealed to Rob that in hell, every good thing given by God has been removed and all that remains is pure evil. The powerful have their powers taken from them and they are unable to remove themselves from the lake of fire. The powers of darkness are there and they hate the souls of mankind because God created mankind in His image, and they hate God. Their anger and demise will burn in their hearts as they torture those who are with them. How sad it is that they will suffer for an eternity for their own pride and selfishness.

Rob sat there and began to think about Art. Jesus knew Rob was beginning to feel sad over Art.

"You're thinking about Art aren't you?" Jesus asked.

"Yes, it's so sad thinking about where he is and what he's experiencing."

"Rob, I am grieved too. Art just wouldn't listen. I gave him every opportunity to turn to Me. He would have nothing to do with Me. This is the consequence of giving mankind freewill. If he had lived another 1,000 years, he still would have not received My gift of salvation. Sometimes I must give them over to their own depravity. I realize that this reality is very hard on you, but it's also hard on Me because I loved Art too, and wanted him to make Me Lord."

Jesus explained, "People are blinded by their own pride in thinking that God doesn't exist, or that We are simply a force in the universe. The lie that Satan perpetrated from the beginning was that God is not who He says He is, and God will not do what He says He will do. We cannot lie, and if we state it, it must be. Therefore, ample warning has been given for each individual to understand what We have revealed would happen to them. When We see people turn from Our truth to the lies of Satan and the world We grieve, just as We celebrate when someone turns to Me for their salvation."

Time with Dad

Rob decided that he needed to spend some time with his dad. After witnessing the final demise of mankind, and the reality of Art in hell, Rob felt as if he needed to talk with his dad about Art.

He asked Jesus if it would be a good thing to discuss Art's life with his dad.

Jesus said, "Your dad wants to grieve with you and has been waiting for the appropriate time to share his heart with you. He and I have had many conversations about Art and I think it's time for the two of you to share your feelings."

Rob found himself in front of a large metallic door. The entrance seemed almost industrial looking and futuristic. Rob knew it was the doorway into his dad's mansion, because his dad always loved modern architecture and the entrance reminded him of an entrance to an elevator. Rob figured it would have a digital code-pad to open it. As he looked, sure enough, the pad was there. He pressed the digital button that read, "Guest." The door slid open into the wall, and his dad was standing there smiling like a little boy.

"Hi Rob, I've longed for this opportunity to visit with you. I have so much to show you, and we need to catch up on all that we've missed being apart."

"That's quite a door there dad," Rob replied.

"You like it?" He asked excitedly. "Jesus prepared it for me and I added the keypad design and Rob, I've also designed many other features that I think you will find interesting. Come in to see my home. I have so much to share with you."

Rob's dad was a mechanical engineer and as a hobby, he invented things in his basement back on earth. He loved tinkering and drawing elaborate devices that he believed would one day change the world. None of his devices ever made it into production, but he didn't seem to mind because it was his passion.

He would often blame the lack of proper equipment that he had access to as the reason why his inventions never made it. His small workshop in their basement was the focal point of the boy's memories and relationship with their dad growing up.

Rob and Art both loved going down there and helping their dad with his gadgets. The shop had a band saw, a lathe, and a drill press. It was amazing to think of all the things Rob's dad made using the antiquated equipment that was there. Throughout the years of inventing things, an array of interesting objects existed. Rob and his brother would try to figure out what they were, as they studied them on the many shelves that lined the workshop. Their dad would never tell them what he was making until it actually worked. So, when it didn't work, he would add it to the other failed inventions on the shelf.

Rob's dad worked for a bathroom scale company and engineered various models of scales for both doctors and home use. His engineering included aspects of both accuracy and esthetics. He loved reinventing new models and boasted about having the most accurate scales on the market. Everyone loved their dad and credited him with the company's success. During the war, he reworked the assembly line, and made a variety of parts for surveillance devises for the war effort. His ingenuity and practical thinking kept everyone employed through all the hard economic times.

He didn't have a formal education, but was brilliant in many ways. He was a great dad and loved his boys. When the boys entered their early teens he had them help him with an invention that he thought would pay their way through college. He created a machine that would test the strength of a man's grip. After placing a penny in the slot, the customer could squeeze the grip and see how strong they are by viewing a dial displaying how many pounds registered.

They placed several machines in various stores across town. Rob's dad thought it would be a simple matter for the boys to collect the money out of the machines. What their dad didn't foresee, is that many of the small machines would disappear due to theft. The machines that weren't stolen frequently broke, leaving them empty. After a year of struggling with the business, he finally gave it up. The boys were thrilled when their dad decided to end the business. They were frustrated over riding their bikes to the various locations, only to find the machines were empty and, or broken.

Their dad always made time for them and took them fishing, hiking, and hunting. They loved spending time with him because he was a "man's man," and taught them how to be men. Art was favored because he was more like his dad than Rob. His athleticism and love of sports gave them a connection that was special. As Art went into early adulthood, their dad seemed to live through Art's many achievements in sports. Rob was never the star, although he tried his best to excel. Most often, he was only an average athlete. Art and their dad seemed to become closer and closer as Art entered college and played competitive college hockey.

As Rob entered his dad's house, he was surprised by the strange objects that were everywhere. The modern mansion reminded Rob of a tall modern skyscraper rather than a home. The crystal flooring in the entry glowed and changed colors as you moved across it. It was subtle and soothing and seemed to have a beauty unique to the home. The objects were a variety of futuristic looking devices that performed various functions. One of the walls projected digital images of family members, taken from his dad's memory. On one wall there were images that captured all the special moments throughout Rob's lifetime. The room had seating that faced each of the walls like a theatre. The walls were faceted at various angels, and on each wall were the memories of each specific member of the family.

"Rob, have a seat," he said, as he gestured to sit facing one of the walls. Highlights from Rob's life played before them. They were all moments that his dad cherished from the past. As he watched himself at various ages, his dad said, "Rob these walls remind me of the important things in a man's life. The images are how I saw you." Some of them are scenes while others are still pictures that captured the moment.

Rob was astounded by the special moments that were seen from his dad's viewpoint. Rob couldn't get over how different they were from his own. Some of his dearest moments were never given a second thought by Rob. It was the little things that captured the heart of the matter. Rob couldn't believe how many wonderful moments his dad had of him. His love for Rob was evident, and it made Rob feel blessed. It was a wonderful experience and the images played on and on without repeating.

His dad didn't need to say anything; the images said it all. "Your mom and I spend a lot of time here talking about you two boys. We are so blessed to have these memories. There are not too many people who have experienced the rich life that your mom and I shared. This wall is just about you, but I have walls throughout the house for every family member and close friends. The images are just the beginning of an eternity of memories that I will continue to place on the walls."

"Come over here," he said. "I want you to watch Art's wall."

The wall was across from Rob's and the images were heart warming, and special, from a totally different perspective. His early life was full of mischief, and their dad enjoyed catching him at his game. Art was a handful, but their dad loved the challenge. He was so cute as a young boy, and it was obvious that their dad thought so too.

As Rob remembered some of the events, he said to his dad, "I never realized that those times were so special to you."

His dad replied, "You two were the center of my life Rob. I cherished so many things that we did together. As I look back upon it, there were some things I wish I would have done differently with Art. Knowing what I know now, my influence in shaping his selfish ambitions and allowing him to obsess over certain pursuits may have contributed to his demise."

"Rob, although we loved Art with all our hearts, his desire to be the center of attention led to his selfishness. I allowed him to pursue his success in sports at any cost. That world, without constraint and limits, became more addictive than any drug. Art's giftedness was the very thing that was his enemy. The world is so seductively deceitful and evil beyond our understanding. Without the Lord to guide us, everyone is susceptible to the lies that promise fulfillment but deliver sorrow and death."

"When I look at the images of Art, that at the time were the sweetest memories for me, I realize that in fact, they may have been the most seductive and deceitful times for him. I now know that the discipline and chastening of the Lord, and for that matter, parents, can be the best memories of all when we look back upon them. Rob, as I see how you struggled and played second fiddle to Art, I believe that it may have been the best thing for you. It's so amazing how the words of the Lord are so true, "the first shall be last and, the last first."

"I'm so glad that even though Art let his self-absorbed life block out God, his life will have an eternal impact on so many others. Through the wealth Art accumulated, God will use much of it to spread the gospel. When I see the sovereignty of God and His wisdom, it makes me content that He is always in control."

"Rob, I never had a chance to thank you for loving your mom and I the way you did and for planting the seeds of salvation that led us to the Lord. The changes we saw in you when you gave your life to Jesus, and your steady faith during trials, allowed us to see our Lord through you. We never realized how empty our lives were until we received Jesus into our lives. We were privileged to share the intimacy you brought to your family. How blessed we are to know that everyone in the family will eventually be here and experience this place with us. Art's life wasn't a product of our lack of love for him. We tried to break through to him so many times. It was a battle won by the enemy, and ultimately, his own undoing."

Rob asked if he could come over from time to time to look at all the memories he had for everyone in the family.

His dad replied, "Of course you can, I would love to watch them with you and discuss the impact that those memories have had on eternity. One thing I've learned by reviewing these memories and then seeing God work through them, is that God uses all these things together for His ultimate purpose. There is nothing that happens that isn't a part of God's plan."

Rob finally got up and said, "Are you ready to show me

the rest of your mansion dad?"

"I'd love that Rob," he replied. "I want you to see my new workshop."

They walked down a long hallway to a large room that had an extensive array of industrial equipment. Milling machines, lathes, presses, drills, saws, and every kind of tool imaginable. The workshop was set up to make anything imaginable.

"Wow!" Rob proclaimed, "I can't believe this place dad! You must be having a ball with all this equipment."

In the shop were two angels working on a project together.

"Rob," he said, "Let me introduce you to Abel and Rael. They help me with my work here. I am blessed to have them. They are incredible at crafting whatever I conceive. The Lord gave them to me to assist in my inventions. I am able to create more things for all my family and friends because they increase my productivity so dramatically. The Lord is preparing me for my work, when we are sent back to the new heaven and earth. He has given me a vision for the utilization of my inventions for everyone there."

Rob's dad was excited as he told Rob that he was able to create anything his mind can conceive.

"Rob," he said, "I am able to clearly visualize how to construct and manufacture inventions without much effort. My mind has an expanded capability that I didn't have before. Jesus explained it to me in terms that I was able to understand. He called it freeing my intellect, by eliminating my flesh. The memory projector is just one of many inventions that I've created here. I love imagining ideas that enrich lives and have purpose. Some inventions are strictly for fun, while others are tools for the production of other people's ideas. I am working on artificial intelligence for robotics that makes mass production possible."

"My mansion is filled with these things, and I am also

creating them for your mom and some of our friends. Your mom says that I'm like a little kid in a candy store. I guess you could say she's right."

On the table was a small box with Rob's name on it.

"What's that" Rob asked.

"Something I've been working on specifically for you."

"Can I open it?" he asked.

"Sure, go ahead."

In the box was a small metallic cube that seemed to have another dimension to it. Rob picked it up and wondered what it was.

"It's a history cube," his dad replied.

"History cube?" Rob asked curiously."

"Yes," his dad explained, "I know how you loved reading books on history and love talking about how America was founded. Your study of the Christian roots that were woven into the country will be enhanced. This cube contains all the events that ever happened throughout history. These events were recorded by Jesus and downloaded for you to experience and enjoy. I have created a holographic projector of the recordings that put you in the center of the event, as if you were there, but invisible to everything and everyone around you. This is much like the experience you have when you open the "Living Word" book. The History Box was made because I knew that you had a love of history. It's my special gift to you, please take it home with you. Would you like to try it out?" he asked. Rob was delighted by the prospects of seeing things like the signing of the Declaration of Independence."

He asked his dad, "What do I do?"

"Sit over here Rob," his dad said.

"What would you like to see?"

Rob immediately said, "The signing of the Declaration of Independence."

As Rob said it, his dad pushed a touch screen on the side.

Rob was immediately surrounded by the images of history playing before him. The scenes were so real; it was like being there in the room with George Washington and the other leaders of his time. Rob was so taken back, that he forgot about how long his dad had been waiting there. Fortunately his dad patiently waited for him to finish. He realized that he would have an eternity to play out all these scenes later.

Rob turned around and saw his dad standing there with a smile on his face and said, "You can turn it off now." As he said, "off" the machine stopped playing.

"That was incredible dad!" Rob exclaimed.

"How did you come up with that invention?" he asked.

"Well, it all started when I was with Jesus, and he was showing me a future event. I asked him how he was able to show a future event. I know that was a stupid question, but he told me that all events past, present, and future are recorded by the Holy Spirit. I asked him if these events could be recorded in a device. He confirmed that they could, but the amount of information would be so enormous that there would be no device yet invented that could hold that much data. That's when I went to work inventing some way to hold a huge amount data. It took me countless experiments to finally figure out how to make the device. What I finally realized is that matter as we understood it on earth only existed in the three dimensions. Matter within those dimensions had limitations, but here the dimensions are limitless. That's what allows us to move about through thought, time and space. By applying additional dimensions to a honeycombed alloy cube and using those added dimensions, I was able to increase the data to the twenty-fourth power. That exponentially increased the data capacity to contain a limitless amount of information."

"The projection was a simple matter once the data could be recorded and stored from the limitless dimensions within a given physical space and time."

Rob seemed overwhelmed by how ingenious his dad was. He shook his head and said, "I never realized how brilliant you were!"

"Rob," he said laughing, "you will find out that we all become geniuses here. Our intelligence is unimpeded. You will soon see how brilliant you are too."

He took Rob to a crystal terrace that extended out over the gardens below and looked in on Rob's mom who was dancing and singing on her terrace.

Rob's dad laughed and said, "She does her dancing every day at this time. I love watching her. She is so fulfilled and happy. Rob, she probably never told you that she always wanted to be a dancer when she was a young girl. Her parents couldn't afford to send her to dancing lessons. Can you believe how well she dances? She is so talented. She often performs at banquets."

"This is all too much Dad. When I danced with mom, it was as if she were a professional. It was an incredible feeling seeing her have so much fun with me. And when I think of her back on earth in that wheelchair, with her crippled joints, I can only think of how great and wonderful our God is. His love for us has no limits."

Rob's dad said, "Let me show you a few of my newer inventions, I think you will find them fascinating." He took him over to what looked like a comfortable recliner. This is my Dream Chair, it converts an idea into a plan. The idea came to me when some of my friends here had some great ideas for inventions, but had no idea how to create or produce them. I believe this is the closest thing anyone has ever come to artificial intelligence."

"This is how it works: a person conceives an idea in their

mind that would enhance their life and / or others. The machine searches their mind for that concept, then it calculates the feasibility of that idea. If the machine calculates that the idea is possible to create, a series of written processes and plans are produced with schematics for a prototype. Sometimes I must add to the idea for the device to make it work. Almost everyone has an idea, and with some help, now they can see their dream realized."

"Here's another invention that allows everyone to make music. I call it "The Composer." Let me put this head piece on you, and I'll show you how it works."

"First, let's start with the songs words. Think of something that has recently moved you."

Rob replied, "let's use, dancing."

"Good Rob," his dad replied. "Now what was it that captured your emotion and moved you abut dancing?"

"It was the joy of feeling the music within my soul and experiencing it, with someone I love very much." he replied.

"Good, let's use those words and let the Composer add to them. We'll sequence them into a methodic format that lends itself to rhythm and melody. Now, let's answer some questions about the type of music you would like it to be," Rob's dad explained.

A list of over 100 choices came up on the device. Rob pressed the words on the screen that said soft rock. Then a list of tempos came up and played as he pressed them. Rob selected a smooth methodical beat that had a deep percussion.

"Now what type of voice would you like?" his dad prompted him.

A list of choices appeared: male, female, high, medium, low, raspy, etc. As he pressed each one, a sampling of the voice was heard.

Rob selected the voice type, and his dad said, "That's it

Two Ways to an End

Rob, the Composer will do the rest."

Rob was amazed as the Composer took what he had input into the device, formatted the music, and created a catchy tune that was exactly what Rob wanted. As the music played and the words were sung, Rob began to sing along. Then he laughed with delight thinking about having talent for music, without really having any talent for music.

"One more device and we will call it a day," his dad proclaimed. "I don't want you to see all my stuff in one day. I want you to come over often, and I'll show you a new invention every time you come."

He took Rob up to a room where he spent time in the Living Word. There was a small table with the Living Word book sitting on it, but there wasn't a chair for sitting which seemed odd to Rob. Instead, there on the floor, was a metal platform that raised the floor about six inches. A matching platform was extended from the ceiling that matched the one on the floor.

"Step up there Rob," his dad said smiling. "Now move to the middle of the platform." Rob's dad then said "float" and as soon as he said the word; Rob was floating in mid air. "This is my environmental simulator, Rob. It's where I experience the Living Word. Rob let me explain what you can do and why it enhances the experience of the Living Word. Have you had a flying experience yet?" he asked.

"Yes," Rob replied, "As a matter of fact I have, as I watched creation in the Living Word."

"Good!" his dad said, gave him additional instructions. "Now what I want you to do, is to assume the position as if you were flying."

Rob flattened his body with his face down as if he were flying. "Wow!" he exclaimed, "I am floating!"

His dad said, "That's exactly right Rob, this machine removes the any confinement, allowing you to float in any position and simulates the environment you are in as it appears before you. I actually find that the position that you're in, and the motion that accompanies it, adds to the experience, as the Living Word appears before your eyes."

Rob's dad handed him the Book, and he randomly opened it to the place where Noah was in the belly of a ship in a fierce storm. He began to rock as if he were there. The waves jolted him back and forth. He felt as if he was moving to and fro with the waves. He was laughing because he knew that the experience wasn't real, but yet it seemed so real.

He closed the book because he was getting sea sick, and as his dad said "simulator off," Rob found himself back on his feet.

"That was a blast Dad. Can you make me one of those?" he asked.

"Sure Rob," he replied, "but you have several people waiting ahead of you. This is an initial prototype and I'm still working out some of the production issues. They won't be available for awhile, Rob. Everyone wants one of these when they experience it. I'll see what I can do to move you up as a priority."

"Sorry Rob, I have to end our time together now," his dad announced, "I have a dinner date with your mom. Please come back tomorrow, and I'll show you some more of my inventions." Then he turned and looked at Rob tenderly, and said. "It's been so rewarding showing you what I love doing and what I've been doing ever since I arrived here. Having you here makes my work so much more meaningful."

Rob hugged his dad and said, "You are very special dad, I am blessed to be your son. I will forever remember this day with joy. I love you so much Dad. Your passion for your work has inspired me to learn how the Lord can use me."

His dad smiled, and said, "Your giftedness is far greater than mine, and Jesus has great plans for you."

New Earth

Rob wanted to spend some time with Jesus. He was in such awe by how fulfilled his dad was here by using his special gifts and abilities. Rob was wondering what special talent his dad was talking about when he said to him "Jesus has great plans for you." He was perplexed and asked himself, what special gift do I possess that could be used by God for a greater purpose. Rob couldn't think of any outstanding talents that he might have.

Rob went up to the room that Jesus had created just for them, and where he knew Jesus would be waiting for him. He couldn't get over how Jesus always knew when he needed him. He understood intellectually that Jesus is omniscient, but to actually see him appear before his eyes every time he thought about Him was something he was having a hard time getting used to.

As he entered the room, there Jesus was, smiling. He knew exactly what Rob was thinking.

"Rob," Jesus said tenderly, "You underestimate your giftedness. I understand that you want to know how you will fit into Our plan. After visiting with your dad, and seeing how his passions and gifts are being used, you want to know how you will be used. Be patient Rob. As time goes on, you will fully understand yours as well. You need to relax and allow Our plan for you to develop."

"Rob, you're very special, and your giftedness is in your connection and love of people. Some people have a specific talent in one area while others have more general talents that make them useful in broader ways. They connect with a wider variety of interpersonal functions and are used to influence a greater sphere of people. You were created to be used in a more general way as a leader. Unlike your dad who has a very specialized and specific talent, and a unique creativity, you also possess very special and unique abilities. People gravitate toward you and simply, love being around you. Back on earth you helped so many young adults discover their roles as husbands, wives, and / or parents. Your ability to see what they could not see is a talent just like your dad's talent even though it's different. In some ways, your talent is more personal, because it expresses, and touches, ones emotional spirit and involves the application of love. Love is the highest attribute given by the Father and has the greatest impact on the Kingdom."

"Do you want to know what your unique gift is? It's love! Love of Us and the love of other people. It's what lights the fire of passion within you. Why do you think that one of your favorite things back on earth was giving gifts? You were created and crafted for giving to others. In doing so, you are fulfilled. I want you to examine yourself and look for ways that you can use your unique talent."

"I had a similar conversation with your father when he first came here. He wondered why any mechanical abilities would ever be needed here. Now he's unstoppable. His giftedness has developed as he exercises and expands the applications for his gifts and talents. He continues to find more and more applications for their use. You will find the same fulfillment with the use your gifts as you seek to develop them."

"I believe that as you hone your gifts, you will become an amazing leader. Your leadership skills will be utilized in so many ways. It will draw many people into your sphere of influence and enrich those to whom you minister to. Your childlike quest for fun and adventure will have a very special influence on people's lives. Rob, don't underestimate your giftedness. We created your unique abilities. Now it's up to you to develop and use them. Many will seek fellowship with you because of your giftedness. Remember Rob, you will reign with me for an eternity." Jesus said.

Rob responded by thanking Jesus for lifting him up and encouraging him. As he thought about what Jesus had said he realized that he needed to trust God's plan for him. He knew that his gifts were not tangible like his dads, so it was difficult to see how they would be used by God. After thinking about it, he knew God's plan would be far better than anything he could imagine and it was his hope that his gifts would bring glory to God.

Jesus knew exactly what Rob was thinking. The pieces of Rob's internal puzzle would soon come together as Rob discovered that everything revolves around relationships. The center and meaning for the existence of all of God's children is in the knowledge that grows in understanding truth and applying it with love.

"Rob," Jesus said, "I want us to take a journey together to reveal to you how you fit into our eternal plan. We will go forward in time and you will get a glimpse of life on the new heaven and the new earth."

Rob knew that he was about to see what would eventually be his eternal home. The anticipation of the new and improved world prompted him to ask Jesus if there would be other worlds similar to earth in the universe. Jesus seemed amused by his question.

Jesus put His arm on Rob's shoulder and said, "Isn't what I created for you here, enough?"

Rob had to think for a moment and as he thought, realized how satisfied he was just to be in the presence of Jesus. Rob was ashamed that his thoughts still clung to the material world rather than the spiritual world which is far more fulfilling. Thinking in terms of the spiritual realm was hard to get accustomed to, even though Rob knew it would give him total fulfillment.

Jesus said, "The wonders that I create in the future will be far better than anything you can imagine. Remember how you never liked to ruin the surprise when your family was trying to figure out what was in the gifts that you gave them?"

"Yes it was the best fun!" exclaimed Rob.

Jesus smiled and said, "Leaving the surprise for all the things that are to come, is the best part for Me, as I see your enjoyment fulfilled. But because you are unsure about your purpose, I will show you a small portion of what We have in store for you. Open the Living Word Rob, and say, "new earth."

As he opened it and spoke, "new earth," he could see that the old earth was being consumed with fire. He then watched the new earth form before his eyes, much like it did during creation. As it formed, the entire surface was covered with lush vegetation, like an elaborate garden filled with spectacular exotic plants. New exotic fruits filled the plants and a fragrant aroma filled the air. Rivers shimmering with crystal clear water meandered through the lush landscape created a soothing sound that drew you into the environment. The limitless varieties of plant life were as numerous as the grains of sand. All things were fresh and healthy, unique and beautiful each in their own specific way.

There were animals everywhere grazing in the gardens,

eating from the plants, and cohabitating with one another. There was a lion, and, lying next to him, was a lamb. The earth was in total harmony, and in tune, with God Himself.

Rob observed the various regions and climates throughout the new earth. He realized that it would take an eternity to explore and discover all of God's wonders created just for those who made Jesus Lord. How privileged he was to experience it before it was actually created.

Rob then saw heaven descend down on the earth and sparkle like a jewel. The celestial city of New Jerusalem glowed and was beautiful as it approached the new earth. The glory of God illuminated the city in a multitude of pure color that magnified its tremendous brilliance. Other cities appeared, but none as magnificent as the New Jerusalem where God would rein on His throne. Rob knew that that this would be his new home. Regardless of where God would send him to serve, New Jerusalem would always be his home. Rob wondered if his mansion would still be there when the time came.

As he thought about it, Jesus said, "I believe you have some questions for me as you see these things unfold."

Rob smiled, and said, "Will things be the same as they are now when heaven comes down upon the new earth?"

"Well," Jesus replied, "Yes and no. Everything is constantly changing and becoming new here in heaven. When the time comes for heaven to come down to the new earth, it will be different because much will have been added to it. It will still be the same in essence, and the Glory of the Father will be present to usher in a perfect environment for His children."

As Rob entered New Jerusalem, he noticed that the city was bustling with activity as people enjoyed perfect fellowship and wonders of God. Everyone knew one another. Every relationship was special with a closeness that was unique and intimate. Rob could see why marriage was unnecessary here. People were in perfect harmony with one another. The love that came from God Himself was flowing through each person, making them like Him. The perfection of lives without selfishness and needs, made service for God's glory a true joy. The common desire to do the Father's will made each person's relationship with God and each other perfectly unified.

Jesus explained that there would be various levels of authority. Each heir would inherit a portion of the new earth to rule. Every person will be in charge of their own estate. Many will oversee a large domain, but, without selfish ambition. There will be commerce and prosperity that is unimpeded by sin. Everyone's motives will be rooted in their love for one another and for doing the will of the Father. With selfishness and pride removed from the new society, everyone will become enriched, without any wants or needs. There will be no pain, no suffering, just joy, laughter, and a sense of purpose in glorifying God. This will be the new culture.

Rob looked and he saw technologies and structures that were more spectacular and magnificent than anything he could have imagined. Rob observed the harmony of everyone living there. Jesus took him in for a closer look at what Rob's specific role would be. They traveled and then entered another beautiful city with tall and magnificent structures. There were parks and gardens similar to those in New Jerusalem. The city was huge, like a major populous in the middle of a giant garden. Water lagoons with streams flowing through them were interspersed throughout the city.

Rob asked, "Where are we?"

"This is the new city of Philadelphia Rob," Jesus replied. This is your city, and it is where you will reign with me."

Rob seemed confused, "you mean I won't live in the New Jerusalem?" he asked.

"Not exactly, you will still have a mansion there, and you will come to visit the Father and those who live there. There will be frequent banquets, and you will spend a considerable amount of time in the celestial city. Philadelphia is where you will lead others and I am entrusting them to you."

Am I a leader, or manager, of something here?" Rob asked.

"No Rob," Jesus replied, "you will be a king."

Rob laughed, and said, "You're kidding."

"No Rob, this is what I've been telling you. You are a beloved leader, and all of the people that you impacted through your ministry on earth, and those that you will impact here, by loving others, will live here with you. Your whole family will come and enjoy the riches that I will provide for you, and everyone who I've entrusted to you. Each one of them will use their giftedness to impact the greater Kingdom and to give glory to the Father. They will all be part of the Royal Family."

As he watched people moving about and enjoying themselves, he was in awe at how beautiful their glorified bodies were. They sparkled with vitality just like Jesus' body and were powerful and illuminated. Their glow was so beautiful that it prompted Rob to want to touch them.

Jesus put His hand on Rob's shoulder and said, "Touching them will be like touching me. You will feel the love of the Father through each of them, just as it does by touching Me. That's why sin doesn't exist here. The love of the Father flows through everyone and everything here. His power is also given to you to create things and enhance life within this environment."

"How do people travel here?" Rob asked.

Jesus tried to explain. "The new earth exists in a dimension that allows physical space to be relative to the spiritual space in other dimensions. By spiritually traveling through one dimension, you're automatically transported to that space in another physical dimension. Rob there are no bounds for the Spirit, it is not physical, and therefore, it does not fall under the laws of physical nature. That's why it appears that one can go through walls. In actuality we're really not going through physical walls. We're moving from one spiritual space to another, and then bringing our physical body into that physical space. That's why in heaven you are free to move from one location to another. Your soul body is not physical, but spiritual."

"Rob, that's what makes these new glorified bodies so incredible. We have created them to be without any physical limits. They are a living organism and have no physical matter. This concept is foreign to any scientific ways that exist on present day earth. For you to fully understand this, you will need to wait until you actually experience it. Once you receive your resurrected body, you will be able to travel the universe and go anywhere you want in a moment. Once you receive your glorified body, you will be without physical limits. This power will allow you, and everyone whose name is written in the Book of Life, the ability to reign with Me throughout the entire universe. There are an infinite number of places and wonders to ever see them all. My creation knows no end, has no limits and is ever expanding. You will enjoy all of it through eternity."

"Your knowledge and understanding will continually expand as you spend more time with Us. You will find purpose and meaning in everything that you do. Our love for you and then in turn your love for others, will never end."

"Can you see why your gift is one of the greatest gifts now?" Jesus asked.

Rob was so taken back that he wasn't sure if what he just saw was real. He wanted to fall on his face before Jesus to express his gratitude for it all.

Jesus looked into Rob's eyes and said, "Rob, you don't

need to say anything, it is my good pleasure to bless you."

As he was taken to the throne of God, he realized what God had intended for mankind and why He created them. Rob joined everyone there worshipping Him and celebrating their unique purpose. Their joy radiated and filled the throne-room.

Crowns were cast before Him as they sang songs and proclaimed His glory. The experience made him want to actually go there himself, to lift up the Lord for revealing these events to him. Rob knew that this was only the beginning of what God would reveal. The joy of knowing Him was beyond his wildest dreams. All he could do was fall down in gratitude for what he had been privileged to see.

Art's Memorial service

It was a typical dreary New York spring day appropriate for the solemn mood of Art's memorial service. As Courtney and her roommate left their apartment, the thought came into her mind that she should read the letter that Rob wrote to his brother. She paused at the stairs leading down to the limo that was waiting for her, and instantly decided that if the letter had such a profound affect on her it might also have that same affect on others. She raced back up to the apartment and pulled the letter out of her Bible where she had put it a couple of days earlier.

Her roommate Rebecca asked why she went back into the apartment, and she explained what she was planning to do at the service. Rebecca was excited that Courtney had decided to share her story and that the gospel of Jesus Christ would be presented at her dad's memorial service.

She hugged Courtney and said, "I'm so proud of how far you've grown in such a short period of time."

It was a short ride to the Chapel that was located in the center of Manhattan's business district. The structure seemed out of place among all the modern skyscrapers. The small chapel was old with ornate features that were gothic looking. From the front, it looked very small and narrow, but once inside, deceiving, due to its enormous depth. Once inside, it felt as if you were in another century where the church was at the center of the people's lives. Courtney selected the Chapel as a tribute because her dad had a love of Manhattan and all that it represented. This chapel stood out in stark contrast to the cold buildings that surrounded it. Her dad's office was right down the street and she could see the building from the chapel.

The ride with Rebecca was to the Chapel was short leaving little time to discuss how she would deliver her message and present the letter. She wasn't sure who would be there, or how it would be received, but what she did know was that the Lord placed it upon her heart to read the letter. Courtney was confident that God had a greater purpose in mind than what she capable of understanding.

As Courtney entered the vestibule of the Chapel, she saw her mom waiting for her to come in. She hugged her and her mom asked how she was doing.

Courtney said, "I'm fine Mom, I have so much to share with you, but with all the arrangements I haven't been able to talk to you about everything that has transpired."

Courtney knew that the subject of her sudden change to Christianity would be a sensitive subject. Her mom was busy with her new marriage and family activities. That left limited time for their relationship, and the added burden of Courtney's heavy load at school furthered their separation. Courtney and her mom were slowly growing apart from one another. They only saw each other over holidays and were rarely able to engage in any deep or meaningful conversations.

When Courtney was younger she had considered her mom to be her best friend. They did everything together and her mom's world revolved around raising her. After Courtney went off to college, the separation left a gap in her mom's life that she eventually filled through a relationship with a man who had four children from a previous marriage. His wife was killed in an auto accident which left him with four children to raise on his own. Courtney was surprised when her mom suddenly decided to marry him after only a couple of months of dating. She seemed genuinely happy with her new responsibilities and the kids seemed to love her. At first Courtney was hurt by the separation, but as time went by, she realized it was the best thing for both of them.

As they looked into each others eyes, tears began to flow as they embraced. Courtney's realization of how hard life can be at times, and how she had never thought about death before gripped her. The reality of knowing that her dad was probably not in heaven intensified her emotions. As she looked at her mom she thought she might not be headed to heaven either. The thought of her mom ending up in the same hopeless situation made her realize how important the letter was. An usher came and asked if he could escort her to her seat. As she walked to the front of the Chapel, she was surprised at how many people were there.

Art knew most all of the investment bankers in New York and had dealings and partnerships with many of them. He was well known for architecting buyouts and mergers and had gained the respect of many high-powered executives. The thought of all the power and wealth represented in one place made her realize that her dad did have a greater purpose than making money. He did affect lives, and she was sure that God would use it for His ultimate purposes.

She sat down, as more people came into the Chapel and reflected on the words she would use as a prelude to the letter. Her training as a lawyer prepared her as if she were building a case. This could be the ultimate case and it might be the only opportunity to present the gospel to each of these influential people.

Courtney knew that the majority of the investment banking community were Jewish and decided that her opening words would be the most crucial in reaching them. It was good that as she sat there, she could organize her thoughts and think about her dad in a positive way. It was if God was supernaturally giving her the words to say. She felt the Holy Spirit's presence. This made any fear she had go away. She prayed that He would speak through her and that the people there would have open hearts to receive God's truth.

The pastor of Courtney's new church home came to the podium and welcomed the family and close friends and then prayed. He asked if any other people would like to speak about Art before his daughter addressed the group.

Adam, Art's partner came to the podium and looked visibly distraught.

"Thank you all for coming to honor Art's life. Art and I had been together for more than fifteen years, and I probably knew him as well as anyone here. We spent most of our time working together and sharing the successes as they came along with disappointments and defeats. As all of you know, Art was a work alcoholic and gave all he had to his business. I admit that his death has made me reexamine my lifestyle and my obsession with my work. Art and I committed 12 to 16 hours a day to our business and we rarely took a break. His sudden death makes me realize that life is short and what happened to Art could easily happen to me. I am approaching my 50th birthday, and now that Art's gone, I can sadly say that my life will never be the same. Art and I shared so many passions. It seemed as though time raced by as we dreamed together, and created bigger and better opportunities.

On the surface Art seemed to be unshakable but underneath it all, he had a heart of gold. He was extremely disciplined and determined in everything he pursued. I know that many of you here can attest to his determination and persistence. Art didn't talk about religion or faith, but respected my Jewish heritage and never questioned me about it. He seemed to dislike even thinking about God. I suspect that I'm like most of you, Art didn't really know if there is a God. I know it's hard for me to see the relevance if He does exist in this world. I, like Art, stopped trying to understand whether there is a God. So it is my prayer that God, if you are there, please be merciful to Art. Take good care of him and tell him that we will miss him here on earth.

After Adam, came Nate, Art's attorney and close friend.

He came up and said, "Art was the most influential person in my life. We would often meet for dinner to discuss his holdings, structures, and legal documents. But that wasn't all Art and I would talk about. He seemed to open up and share his heart with me. I'm not sure he would want me to tell you some of the things that he told me in confidence, but what I am convinced about is the fact that he would want you to know that he wasn't as uncaring as most of you think."

"Often times, the veneer of doing business shadows the deeper meaning and purposes of life. He would often share the regrets he had with what he called "reckless pride in himself," that left a wake of ruined relationships. He said that the more he seemed to try and change, the more he seemed to wreck the very thing he wanted to fix. He often talked about reconciling relationships with his ex-wives, and most of all, with his daughter whom he loved very much. Art had a hard time showing love, and even a harder time showing any emotion at all. He often asked me why he couldn't seem to outwardly express what he felt inside. He was much more tender inside than he was outwardly."

"I know that many of you are here today because you respected him and he helped you make a lot of money in your businesses. This was true, he was a genius at putting together business deals. But I also want you to recognize that he never did a deal that he thought wasn't for the betterment of the companies or investors involved. He truly liked to create opportunity that didn't exist. I will miss him because I believe Art was good for me, and I believe, he was good for society. Art had a goodness that was invisible to most everyone who knew him."

The pastor returned and asked if there was anyone else who would like to speak, but no one came forward. He then introduced Courtney.

As she came up and looked out into the Chapel she could see that the Chapel was almost filled to its capacity. She thought that it might have been due to an article that the Wall Street Journal ran on Friday about her father. The article announced that there would be a memorial service for him at the Chapel. She could feel her heart beating as she began her story.

"Most of you knew my father, Art, as a powerful and driven businessman, and that he was. But I also remember him as a fun dad who loved adventure. When I was young, my dad liked to take me to the beach where we played in the sand and made castles. I loved him so much that I wouldn't go to sleep until he came and tucked me in at night. Often times that ended up being pretty late because you never knew when he would be coming home. My dad also was very generous with me and called me his little princess. When I was young I actually thought I was. As the years went by, my dad seemed to be more and more consumed with his work and less with my mom and myself. I know that he never intended to be neglectful, but that was the reality of our life."

"As I look back upon the loneliness and pain caused by my parents divorce, I can see the good that it brought into my life. Had we not been separated, I believe I would have been spoiled and selfish. As I look back, I see how that painful time matured me. I know now that pain yielded perseverance and tenacity as a result of the adversity. It's unfortunate that relationships often end in anger and frustration. As a young adult, I seemed to drive my dad away. I regret that I let my anger rob me of the love I could have experienced knowing him better."

"My dad had a brother who was very close to him growing up. They were inseparable and did everything together. Sometimes life has a way of creating separation to those who are closest to us. As flawed human beings, we often let our pride rob us of that intimacy."

"Since my dad's death, I have vowed to make some changes in the relationships that are, and will be, in my life. I can now see more clearly how God can use me. I am convinced that God would like to have that same change of heart with each of you, as he has with me. The reason that I know this is because I am here today a different person than I was a week ago."

"Last week when I received word about my dad, and saw him there in the hospital helpless, alone, and unconscious, I realized that he had no control over his life. Most of us live in the past or in a state of anxiety over what will happen in the future. I am trying to live for the moment and make wise choices that will determine my new path in life. I am learning to leave the past behind and not worry about tomorrow because tomorrow will take care of itself. Many of you take risks that are rooted in your ability to control the future. Most often, that future is unknowable and outside of your control. I believe that God controls much more than we think He does, and we need to place our trust in Him."

"That brings me to why I feel led to address those of you who are here. Some of you are my family, and I care about you, and love you. My dad's brother Rob also cared deeply for my dad and wrote him a letter expressing that love. My dad never received the letter because he died while it was in route to him. When I was going through my dad's mail, I came across this letter and read it. I broke down and cried out to God to help me. I instantly knew that everything that was expressed in the letter was true and that my dad's brother wrote it in love. I am going to read the letter to you today. It is my hope, and prayer, that it will change your life as it has mine."

The Letter

Dear Art,

As you know, I am entering the final chapter of my life. Spending time lying here in bed has allowed me to reflect upon my life and especially upon my relationships with those I love. Recently, I have been thinking about our younger years together. As I reflect upon them, it brings so many great memories to mind. Our childhood days were filled with a closeness that made us inseparable. I know somewhere down deep, our brotherly love still exists as it once did when we were young. I've realized that our separation has been the only major regret I have in my life. I have failed in keeping our relationship strong and growing through the years.

I can remember the great adventures we experienced together. The winter sledding, the ice hockey, the baseball games, the pretend wars, the fishing, the scary stories, the campfires, the hiking, the tree houses, the wrestling, the races, the hunting, the inventing, and the mischief. What rich experiences we shared.

Remember when dad took us camping and the three of us were lying on the ground looking up at the stars and pointing out the constellations? It was one of the best times of my life, as we took in the wonder of the universe and shared stories with each other. That weekend was one of those times I'll never forget.

It was great having you as my brother and my best friend. I have thought about it often. There were so many times that I felt that way, but didn't say it. As we grew up, you made me feel special and loved. Your courageous and daring personality impacted me in so many ways.

When I think of how you pushed me and made me take risks, it makes me realize how very important you were in shaping my life. I know that at times, I may have been a burden to you, as I tagged along. It's funny how

Larry Babka

at the time, these things, never occurred to us. I never realized the impact they had on me until recently.

Even when we were older, you stuck up for me and then taught me how to stand up for myself. I remember all the double dates, the parties, the dances, the nights out with the guys, and all the times that you let me hang out with you. You were my idol, and I thought the earth revolved around you. Thank you for being there for me and being the best brother a boy could ask for.

How foolish I have been when I think about all the years that have gone by, because I failed to love you unconditionally and nurture our relationship. Art, the one thing I would like to ask you is that I would be able to see you before I pass away. The doctors have given me less than a month to live, and the pain killers are making my consciousness less frequent.

This letter is my last chance to tell you how I feel, because I am unsure I will have another opportunity to see or talk with you again. I need to ask for another favor Art. As I reflect on my regrets, the deepest regret I have is how I presented my change to Christianity to you. I was selfish and judgmental. I didn't think about how it must have seemed from your point of view. How foolish I have been to expect you to understand what I believe, and then just accept it as the truth. My approach was exactly the opposite of what I should have done. As someone who loves you as much as I do, I should have done better.

I am now going to explain what happened in my life that made me rethink the path I was on and why I could no longer stay on it. Please, I am asking at this point to hear me out. This is coming straight from my heart and is my last attempt to reconcile our paths. It is my belief that even though I may only have weeks left here on earth, I will have an eternity to spend with those I love in another world. I so want you to be there with me.

I never told you this, but you may remember the night you and I went to that wild fraternity party on Halloween and drank ourselves into oblivion. Well that night, I went home with a girl who I had dated a couple of times but really didn't care about or even know all that well. You may remember her; she was a tiny blond with short hair. Her name was Rachel. Anyway, I can't remember the details of the evening, because I was out of control drunk. The next morning when I woke up with her, she told me that I told her that I was in love with her, and that I had proposed marriage to her. I had no memory of it at all, and I told her she must have been dreaming. She began to cry, and I could tell she really thought I was serious about being in love with her. She became very distraught when I told her I was drunk and would never marry her. It was cruel and tactless, and it made me realize how selfish I had become.

Long story short, she started stalking me and showing up wherever I was. At first it flattered me, but then she showed up while I was on a date. The next day I called her and told her to stop following me and that I wasn't attracted to her at all. She began to cry, and then I said," Besides, I'm in love with someone else." It was a lie, but I just wanted her to go away. I found out a week later, that she committed suicide that afternoon. I never told anyone because I felt responsible. That day has haunted me every day of my life.

I was depressed and found myself hating who I was. It hit me like a ton of bricks that, in fact, I didn't care about anyone but myself. One night while I was depressed and down, my roommate sensed that something was wrong with me and asked me if I needed to talk. He was a Christian, and asked me if I would like to go with him to a coffee shop where some of them met weekly. I reluctantly agreed and as I look back upon it now, I realize I needed to tell someone what happened.

I didn't tell you because I thought you would think I was a wimp, but it was eating me up inside, and I knew you were so much stronger than me. I didn't open up during the first several meetings with them, but there was something different about them. They all seemed to be so joyful. On the fifth meeting, I told them about the girl and what happened. They didn't judge me or tell me that I was a terrible person. As I kept meeting with them I began to understand that they were not religious or perfect, but rather that they had a relationship with God that was personal. I began to read and understand what was in the Bible. As time passed, I finally came to a place where I believed the evidence and claims made by Jesus were really true. I finally asked Jesus Christ into my heart, and my life began to change. I was so excited about my conversion, I never considered how it would repel those who knew me and were in my life before that change. I now know that it was my immature understanding of what was happening to me that separated me from so many people, including you. I should have expressed myself more lovingly now that I look back upon it.

Art, all that time when I shut you out, you must have thought that I abandoned you. How awful I feel about the whole thing. If only I would have leveled with you and let you in on my internal struggle. It might have kept us together and even closer. I failed you as a brother, but I am hopeful and believe God will mend those wounds. I am turning to you in love so we can be reconciled. How I wish I could do it over; how I would do it different.

This failure has been a secret sin that I have concealed from you and most everyone until now. It's time for me to bring it out into the light and be free of the guilt that I feel. You can continue to shut me out as I did you, because I deserve it, but I will continue to keep my heart completely open to you with every breath. I will pray for you each day until I'm gone, and that is my promise.

Art, I too was very skeptical and found myself wanting to dismiss the whole Bible thing as rubbish. I figured that God had little to do with me and my life. My room mate challenged me to investigate for myself the facts before I dismissed it as untrue. I spent two months trying to prove to myself that it wasn't true. I really wasn't excited about turning my life over to a God I knew little about, and based on what I did know, I realized it would force me to change my behavior.

I wasn't looking to surrender my life to anyone or anything and besides, I was so young; so why worry about it now. I tried to logically dismiss my thinking and behavior as, who I was, and that I would never be able to change it anyway. My selfishness made it very difficult to really dig in and check out the truth. The real reason was that I really didn't want the truth, only an excuse for what I did. However, I needed to really know the truth, so I spent several months trying to disprove the validity of Jesus and the Bible.

I now must try to tell you what it is that I learned, and I'm continuing to learn as a result of my beliefs. These are truths that I believe can change your life forever if you will only keep an open mind and let me explain. That is the right word, it is forever. What I mean and have learned is that "everyone" will pass from this life and live spiritually in another world forever.

The Bible is clear about two places. They are heaven and hell. I know it's about at this stage where you are thinking, "not this heaven or hell bunk again". Please hear me out before you dismiss it. I have studied the facts and after weighing the evidence, found all of it to be true. I would like an opportunity to present these facts to you before you dismiss them. After you hear the evidence and weigh the facts, then you can reject it, but I implore you to please, at least, hear the facts.

First the universe cries out that there is a creator. Look closely at the wonder of nature. Each plant, each animal, each landscape. When you look closely at the intricacy and variety, it is impossible to think that these things randomly appeared. It's like saying that the wristwatch you are wearing was made through an explosion or by chance. The things all around us scream creator. Once you accept that, it's much easier to see God everywhere. How wonderful and intricate we are as humans. Can you remember when your daughter was born? I watched you as you examined her, found her to be so unbelievable as you held her at Mom's house. I can remember it like it was yesterday. The Bible says; "the world displays the Glory of God." and also, "the rocks will cry out at the glory of God, so that none is without excuse".

I know the whole concept of God and His Son is hard to wrap your head around. Please let me try to explain it in a way that makes sense. God has always existed and is one God. But God has three distinct persons within Himself. These in human terms (which are limited) are described as the Father who is the basis of all things and regarded in position but not attributes above the other two persons he initiates. Then there is the Son, He is the expression of God and became a man, (I will explain that later) so that we can rightly relate to God through Him, He is the implementer. Then there is God the Holy Spirit. He is the active component of God that works in everything and provides our ability to connect with Him on a spiritual level. He is the empowerment of God. These three Persons are all equal in power, have the same attributes and are perfection. They are seen and made known to us through their creation, their ongoing works, and through their Word, which is the Bible.

When God created the universe, He created man in His own image. That means that man has a spirit and a soul, and not just a body. The soul and spirit never die. They exist after our physical bodies wear out. As a result of our selfishness and disobedience, we are separated from Him. God is not able to receive or accept anything before Him that is impure because He is Holy and nothing impure, or unclean can exist before Him. The only way for God to receive and accept us in our unclean state is by blood sacrifice that atones for the sin. That's why before Jesus Christ came to earth and died for us, the Jewish people who were God's chosen people, killed animals as a substitutionary replacement for their own death.

Physical life comes from our blood, and only the shedding of blood can atone for the punishment we deserve. That punishment is physical death and separation from God permanently. That requires confinement to a place of spiritual death and isolation. That place is called hell, and Art I can tell you with complete certainty that it does exist.

That is why I must warn you, because I care so very much for you that I am now pleading with you to consider what I am presenting, and then investigate for yourself these truths.

When Jesus came in the form of a man, He became like us, a physical man but lived a sinless life. Jesus was conceived through a woman but was joined with the Holy Spirit of God to become fully God, yet fully man. God's plan to redeem man made His sacrifice complete and final for all who embrace Him. Because He was sinless, while tempted in every way that man can be tempted, He was able to be a substitute for man's sin for eternity. That substitution is called imputed righteousness and allows access to God through His death. His unjust execution, His suffering, His humiliation, and the most horrific execution known to man was the only way anyone could become rightly received by God. That imputed righteousness allows forgiveness to those who have received His free gift of eternal life to become children and heirs of God.

That transaction takes place through a process of belief. Belief that Jesus was conceived through the Holy Spirit and born of a woman. That He grew and lived a sinless life here on earth, and that He is who He said He was, that is, the Son of God.

The Bible predicted His coming, and there are over 324 prophecies precisely fulfilled about where He would come from, His earthly blood line, His persecution, death and resurrection. To fulfill only 48 of those prophecies would be 1 in 10 to the power of 157, or 10 with 157 zeros after it. In other words, the probability of Jesus Christ fulfilling 48 prophecies is the same as one person being able to pick out one electron out of the entire mass of our universe!

 I Believe that Jesus is God, and that He died a physical death so that we can come to faith in Him. We receive His gift of eternal life by accepting that gift. When we accept those truths and accept the gift, we are reconciled with God forever. We receive the third person of the trinity, the Holy Spirit, and He lives within us. Our life is changed as a result of our faith, and we are then received by God as His children. As children, we are heirs to eternal life with Him in heaven. Only those who are reborn in Jesus Christ will be saved from the eternal separation from Him which is hell.

Jesus described hell as eternal suffering and torture. He told a parable about a man who went to hell and went through incredible pain and suffering. The man wanted to warn his family about the place because it was beyond horrible, and he could not escape from the fire and torture.

In Genesis 1:27, it says: "So God created man in His own image, in the image of God He created him, male and female He created them."

But man sinned by disobeying God and they ate from the tree of life that was forbidden by God. So we are born into sin and because of our sin, we are separated from God. In Isaiah 59:2 it says; "But your iniquities have separated you from your God; and your sins have hidden His face from you, so that He will not hear."

Everyone has sinned and are guilty. In Isaiah 53:6, it says: "All we like sheep have gone astray; we have turned, every one, to his own way; and the Lord has laid on Him the iniquity of us all." Also, in Romans 3:23, it says: "For all have sinned and fall short of the glory of God."

The result and penalty of sin is death. God

told Adam and Eve that the penalty of them disobeying His command would be death. It says in Roman 5:12 that: "Therefore, just as through one man sin entered the world, and death through sin, and thus death spread to all men, because all sinned."

But because Jesus came and died on the cross, we can have eternal life through Him. It says in Romans 6:23: "For the wages of sin is death, but the gift of God is eternal life in Christ Jesus our Lord. It is His gift to us to receive."

After death, we are judged. It says in Hebrews 9:27 and 28: "And as it is appointed for men to die once, but after this the judgment, so Christ was offered once to bear the sins of many. To those who eagerly wait for Him, He will appear a second time, apart from sin, for salvation." He is our substitute for the penalty of sin.

God loves us and wants us to be united with Him. To reconcile our sin, He sent His Son. It says in John 3:16: "For God so loved the world that He gave His only begotten Son, that whoever believes in Him should not perish but have everlasting life." Jesus is the only way to have eternal life and our only hope for salvation. In John 14:6, He said: "I am the way, the truth, and the life. No one comes to the Father except through me."

His death and resurrection reconciled us to God the Father. It says in 1 Peter 3:16: "For Christ also suffered once for sins and the just for the unjust, that He might bring us to God, being put to death in the flesh but made alive by the Spirit." It's God's gift of love. It says in Romans 5:8, "But God demonstrates His own love for us, in that while we were still sinners Christ died for us."

We become sons of God and are heirs when we receive His spirit through accepting His gift of salvation. It says in Romans 8:14: "For as many are led by the Spirit of God, these are the sons of God." Then in Romans 8:15: "For you did not receive the spirit of bondage again to fear, but you received the Spirit of adoption by whom we cry out, Abba, Father." It is our acceptance and belief in Jesus that makes us His adopted children through Jesus Christ.

That gift is not earned, it is a free gift. It says in Ephesians 2:8 and 9, "For by grace you have been saved through faith and not that of yourselves; it is the gift of God, not of works, lest anyone should boast." We can never be good enough to earn salvation. In Titus 3:5 and 6 it says; "not by works of righteousness which we have done, but according to His mercy He saved us, through the washing of regeneration and renewing of the Holy Spirit."

That means that our eternal life comes only from and by Jesus Christ. It says in 1 John 5:11-13: "And this is the testimony: that God has given us eternal life, and this life is in His Son. He who has the Son has life; he who does not have the Son of God does not have life. These things I have written to you who believe in the name of the Son of God, that you may know that you have eternal life, and that you may continue to believe in the name of the Son of God." and also in John 1:12, it says: "But as many as received Him, to them He gave the right to become children of God, to those who believe in His name."

Jesus proclaimed that He held the power to grant eternal life. It says in John 5:24: "Most assuredly, I say to you, he who hears my word and believes in Him who sent me has everlasting life, and shall not come into judgment, but has passed from death to life."

To gain salvation, you must believe and confess the Lordship of Jesus Christ. It says in Roman 10:9: "that if you confess with your mouth the Lord Jesus and believe in your heart that God has raised Him from the dead, you will be saved." That is our basis for salvation.

Jesus is waiting for you to receive his free gift. It says in Revelation 3:20; "Behold, I stand at the door and knock. If anyone hears my voice and opens the door, I will come in to him and dine with him, and he with Me."

Art, the question is: are you ready to let Him into your heart? He will change your life. You will never again wonder if you have eternal life. Please consider the cost of not accepting the gift. The separation from God is horrid, and beyond any words could describe. Please bow before Him, and tell Him that you do believe in Him and that you would like to make Him the Lord of your life. Tell Him that you accept His gift of righteousness and that you would like Him to change you.

If you are ready, Jesus is waiting. This simple prayer to the Lord will change your life forever if you pray it earnestly and believe in the words prayed.

Larry Babka

"Lord, I know I am a sinner and unable to live up to the standard you have set as a Holy God. Lord, I believe that You sent Your Son Jesus Christ in the form of a man. I believe he was conceived through the Holy Spirit and from a virgin woman. His name is Jesus, and He is your only begotten Son. He lived a perfect sinless life, although tempted in all things, then suffered, died for me on the cross, and rose from the dead on the third day, that I might be reconciled for my sins. I believe that He is God and now stands at Your right hand. I want to make Him Lord in my life, and I accept His free gift of salvation. Thank you for receiving me, and making me Your child."
Amen

Please call me soon; I will be waiting for you. I love you, and will pray for you daily.

Your brother and best friend,
hopefully forever,
          Rob.

Good Endings

When Courtney finished reading Rob's letter one could have heard a pin drop. As she looked out into the small group of mourners, she could see that many were weeping and impacted by the words. Courtney knew that many of them were headed toward eternal damnation. Courtney held the letter up and told the group that the letter, although never read by her Dad, had changed her life.

Courtney explained, "When I first read this letter, I knew immediately that there had to be a greater purpose in this tragedy. It was as if God Himself was speaking to me. The day that I had to make the decision to remove my father from life support was very difficult. Even though I knew it was the right decision, I was afraid it would haunt me forever without God's intervention. I reread the letter that night and began to weep. I knew my life was headed in the same direction as my father's."

She then paused with tears in her eyes and said, "At the end of it all, what did all of my dad's wealth and power bring him? I made a vow to God that night to make my life count for something more than my personal pleasures and accomplishments."

"When I entered my dad's penthouse apartment, the stark reality of that large cold space made me realize how empty his life was. For all his pursuits and aspirations of control, in the end he couldn't control anything. I have prayed that this letter would impact you, as it has me. It is my sincere desire that each of you consider what you have heard here today, and that you too will examine the path you are on."

"My path has already made me realize that the riches and fulfillment from a life well lived for Jesus Christ are far more exciting and rewarding than any personal gain I could receive from the pursuits of the world. I am so fortunate that this letter reached me now, while I am young and can do something with it. It will be my joy to work for God in all that I do."

As Courtney put her hands over her heart, she said, "I know that this letter may not change your life, as it did mine, but what I do know is that my father's life although at times hard on many of us, did make a difference. God works in amazing ways to get our attention. It is my hope that this may be your wake up call, as it was mine. I can only thank God for His grace and patience. Remember, it's never too late to receive God's gift, I pray today will be that day for you."

After Courtney stepped down from the podium, the pastor of City Assembly came forward and asked if anyone would like to give their life to Christ. By raising their hand they would acknowledge the free gift offered by Jesus.

It was several minutes before the first person raised their hand. The Pastor paused in silence giving everyone enough time to examine their hearts. Then another raised their hand and another, and then several more.

Twelve came to faith in Jesus Christ that day including Courtney's mom and Art's business partner, Adam. Many of the others who were there seemed as though they wanted to raise their hand, but just weren't able to make a commitment. As the Pastor prayed with them and asked if they understood what they were committing to, tears of joy were flowing freely from most everyone. It was obvious God was in their midst, and that many lives would be changed forever.

The next day, Courtney met with her father's attorneys and discussed how her father's assets would be used for God's purposes. Her father's attorney gave his life to Christ at Art's memorial service and understood what Courtney was asking. They worked for several days on setting up a foundation that would allow Art's assets to be used for great things. Courtney was thankful that God would change the heart of her father's attorney, so he could help her, in pursuing God's will.

Two weeks later, they assembled leaders from the various holdings together, including Art's partner Adam, to announce her intentions and plans. Courtney's mom was present along with Art's former wives. Everyone was surprised that Courtney, had invited them all to meeting. Courtney figured it would be best for everyone concerned if she laid everything out completely before them. That way, if there were any questions or issues, they could be addressed at that time. For many, the new structure would sever their involvement. Courtney prayed that the announcement of her plans would be well received.

Courtney looked out into the group and said convincingly; "As most of you know, my father had substantial holdings in many enterprises. I have met with his attorneys and the other members of the family to determine how to proceed in setting up a foundation where these assets can be used for a much greater purpose. One of his largest holdings was in publishing where he held the controlling interest in one of the nation's largest publishing companies. As a powerful vehicle for communication, we will be examining how to best use that holding for the cause of Christ. Many of you will join me in this new foundation as board members. Thank you for your consideration and understanding. I look forward to meeting with each of you individually and discussing your involvement"

Looking Back

It's been almost a year since that day when the letter was read, and as I look upon all the events I've witnessed as God's messenger, I can only marvel at how He works all things together for His good purposes. As Rob's guardian angel, I know how important this story is to him. I have been with him since birth, and have been privileged to see a life well lived for the Father.

Rob asked me to record these events and place them in the mind of this writer. For the families who have been impacted by Rob's life, he wants them to know that it is God who uses a person's life for His Glory. People are vessels and can only be filled with His goodness when they are emptied of themselves. It is Rob's desire that His story will be shared with many and that lives will be turned to Jesus. His prayer is that no person would perish, and that all would turn, and receive God's free gift of eternal life.

Rob is enjoying each moment in heaven and continues to be filled with wonders beyond comprehension. He now understands that the words in Scripture describing the wonders of God are surely true. He desires that each of you look and live for the promises that are only found in a life given to Jesus.

The eternal consequence of your choices will determine the path that you will take. Remember, the path to eternal damnation and destruction is wide. The path to eternal righteousness and fulfillment is narrow. Choose wisely, because you only have the opportunity while you are on earth. There are no second chances after we die, and God desires that everyone would choose Jesus as Lord while alive on earth.

This past year has been filled with joy in seeing lives that were once doomed for separation from God, become children of God, and then for them to be used in great ways. Courtney started the Christian Legacy Foundation ministering to millions of people in third world countries where Christians are persecuted. Her organization has been responsible for starting more than 100 Churches. Courtney is using her legal practice to impact governments worldwide.

Art's partner Adam is now the president of the publishing company, and Courtney's foundation continues to be the largest shareholder. The company has reorganized and is focused on publishing books by Christians who often can't get published by secular publishers. A film division has been formed that will specialize in "Movies With A Message." Their goal is to offer wholesome movies that impact lives for a greater purpose.

Kate published Rob's letter and has given away or sold over 100,000 copies in 9 languages. She also speaks at church memorial services where she shares Rob's letter. She has spoken at 12 memorial services throughout the United States and plans to use the letter to reach people worldwide. More than 10,000 souls have been saved from the impact of the letter and turned their lives over to Jesus Christ. Rob knows that it was God who placed the burden on his heart to write the letter. As he sees what has transpired, and anticipates what God will do in the future, he can only proclaim that all glory goes to God.

Rob's prayer is that like a contagious disease, people will look for opportunities to be used by God, and act upon them. His message to each of you is simple. Make yourself open and available to the promptings of God. It's the small things by ordinary people that often have the greatest impact. The common events of one's life, are used by God so that no man can boast. Rob knows that he is proof that God can, and does, use ordinary people for extraordinary things. May you be blessed and empowered to live your life for God and His purposes.

Epilogue

First, I would like to thank my wife Lenore, who for the past year endured the countless hours in the evenings, and weekends as I worked to finish this book. Her patience was sacrificial as I poured myself into my writing. I would also like to thank all of my family and friends for reading, editing and making suggestions for this book. A special thank you to; Glori Nuessle, Doug Milligan, Doug Coke, and several others, who helped me with the editing, and to my daughter Kimberly, for creating the graphics, and formatting the book.

Most of us go through life with dreams and aspirations that are never realized. I would like to encourage everyone who has a dream worthy of God's calling to stop thinking about it, and just do it. For me, that has been at times a stumbling block in my life. As I think back upon all the things that I could have accomplished for Christ and His calling, I regret that I didn't take more opportunities for Him. But God is good, and I am trusting that He isn't quite done with me yet.

This book is fiction. The characters are fiction, the graphic descriptions are from my imagination. But what I want to make clear is that the foundations of the Christian faith are found within this book, and I have tried to stay true to the Scriptures. Who can know God? He is incomprehensible and beyond our ability to know or understand Him. Regardless of what one writes about the incredible attributes of God, they pale in comparison to what He is in reality. My prayer is that each reader will find the joy and richness that can only be found in a relationship with Jesus.

Now that I am entering the later years in my life, it is my prayer and heart's desire that God would use me in a way that will have an eternal impact and purpose. I am trusting God to do great things with the small talents and gifts that He has entrusted to me. Whatever the outcome of this writing, and any future writings I may pursue, I know that it is unto Him for His glory. It is my prayer that this book will be used by Him for His purposes, whether small or large, and that it will change lives.

I believe this book is spiritually inspired. By that I mean in of myself, I could not have written this book. You see, I am an ordinary guy who has never written anything more than some business letters and proposals here and there, and it has never been a life long dream to write a book. The idea and decision came to me abruptly during my daily morning quiet time with God. I know that may sound strange, but that's how it happened.

God suddenly placed an idea and desire upon my heart to write this book, and I knew immediately what it would be about.

 My prayer is that this book will reach people in a relevant way. I feel strongly that we need more books that promote God's desire for a deep relationship. This book is my attempt to present truth in a manner that will invoke personal reflection and analysis. If those who read it, are led to further investigate the truths of the Bible, and to reflect upon what is presented here, then I have accomplished what I set out to do.

This book formed in my mind as a result of my studies in the Scripture and through prayer. My motivation in writing this book is rooted in a deeper desire for God to use me as I enter my later years coupled with the sorrow I feel knowing how many people are headed toward eternal separation from God. It has been a humbling experience to witness how God is able to work through me, and place ideas in my mind, that I believe convey His heart.

It is my belief that the essence or core of this writing comes from, and has been created and formed by, the Holy Spirit who lives in me, and through me. It is He who has inspired my words, and presented His truth.

These ideas expressed about Heaven may be the figments of my imagination, and in actuality, different than the reality of those events, ideas, or places. But this I do know, whatever I can conceive in my mind will never compare to the riches that await me in heaven. The reason I am certain of that is that it is promised in Scripture.

Although this book is fictional, and the characters and places are imaginary, the reality of a real Heaven and a real Hell are true. It is my sincere prayer that this book would reach millions of lost souls however, if God chooses to change only one life with it, then it will have been well worth it to me.

I am not a great evangelist like some. My gifts are more practical and invisible, but none the less, useful to the body, which is the Church. Most people I believe fall into my category of giftedness and feel like they fail to present and promote the gospel to the world.

The characters in this story are not real people. For example, the characters of Rob and Art are actually a combination of the good and dark areas within my own heart and mind. That is to say, Rob and Art are really both a part of me and many other people I meet and know. None of these characters came from any single person in my life. All the characters are combinations of people everywhere and have no specific meaning or significance. I created the characters from common threads that run though all our lives. My hope is that you will see yourself in the characters in some way, good or bad, and seek to live a richer and more fulfilling life for Jesus Christ.

Lastly, I would like to dedicate this book to my little granddaughters, Hannah and Emma. They are the greatest gift any man could ever ask for and they are so very precious to me. Even more so, they are more precious to God who has a perfect love.

It is my prayer and desire that they will find their path in living lives rooted in the greater purposes that are revealed in a relationship with Jesus Christ. I believe that long after I am finished here on earth, they will make their lives count for a greater purpose which is in the desire to do God's will. May He be Glorified!

Thank you Lord, for placing this burden upon me, may it be used for Your Glory.
AMEN

You too can have a copy of Rob's letter by going to:
www.twowaystoanend.com

The letter can be downloaded in a Word document for personalization. By altering the content to specifically speak to that person, you will be presenting your own version of Rob's letter.

We have also provided a form with specific information for those who would like us to write the letter for you that fits your specific situation. By filling out the questionnaire: we can compose the letter that uniquely speaks to the person you are giving it to. We will put the letter on high quality water mark paper and insert it in a beautiful folder. The web site shows how the final copy is sent. My goal is to give you a tool that will express your heart toward someone you love, so they do not end up as Art did, in hell. God bless you for taking the time to read this story, I pray that it will change your life.

To order a custom letter to a friend or family member, go to:
www.iwroteyouthisletter.com

To order additional books, go to:
www.twowaystoanend.com

To learn more about New Genesis Publishing go to:
www.newgenesispublishing.com

To learn more about the distribution and how you can publish your own book go to: **www.intermediapub.com**

To learn more about the author go to: **www.larrybabka.com**